# EXPERT PROFILES
## VOLUME 4

Conversations with Influencers & Innovators

# EXPERT PROFILES
## VOLUME 4

Conversations with Influencers & Innovators

Featuring

Greg Kristan

Kendra Seck

Don Dodds

Rosemary Frank

Randy Gonigam

Ron Golembieski

Robert Kerr

D.A. Garcia

Christian Fautz, JD

Royalties from the Retail Sales of "Expert Profiles" are donated to Global Autism Project

**AUTISM KNOWS NO BORDERS;**
FORTUNATELY NEITHER DO WE.®

Global Autism Project 501(c)3, is a nonprofit organization which provides training to local individuals in evidence-based practices for individuals with autism.

Global Autism Project believes that every child has the ability to learn and their potential should not be limited by geographical bounds.

The Global Autism Project seeks to eliminate the disparity in service provision seen around the world by providing high-quality training to individuals providing services in their local community. This training is made sustainable through regular training trips and contiguous remote training.

You can learn more about Global Autism Project by visiting GlobalAutismProject.org.

# Table of Contents

# Technical SEO and The Power of Bing

Do you need more traffic to your website? Of course. Who wouldn't? But, have you noticed that it is getting harder to get that traffic with Google's continued updates and algorithm changes? You try to keep up, but no matter how hard you try there is always someone at the top that keeps getting all the good targeted traffic. There are a lot of myths, misconceptions and misinformation about getting traffic from the internet and it may seem like it's hard to master, but it is not. Not when you know the things the search engines are looking for to rank your site first.

Greg Kristan, owner of TM Blast helps small to medium size businesses drive more traffic and leads to their business through Search Engine Optimization. His business is in Cambridge, Massachusetts, and he focuses on good technical SEO as well as giving much attention to Bing and their webmaster tools.

# Conversation with Greg Kristan

*Tell us a little bit more about yourself and how you got started with search engine optimization.*

**Greg Kristan**: I got into SEO way back in 2011. I had two roommates who were photography majors who were trying to get more clients for their wedding photography business. I helped build the website for them and then I did a lot of Google Adwords to promote their services. I discovered organic search along the way, and I fell in love with the ability to drive the right people to the website for free. We were able to land a gig with Make a Wish Foundation out in Providence Rhode Island through SEO, so I wanted to make this a career.

*What type of clients do you help? Do you have any preferences on what type of businesses you work with?*

**Greg Kristan**: I like to work with somebody who has a strong passion for their line of work. Their love for what they do gets me even more excited about helping them drive new leads to their business. I enjoy working in different fields because I get a new appreciation for what someone else is trying to achieve. So, if you are passionate about what you are trying to accomplish, I'm on board.

*What kind of problems do you see clients having? Why do they come to you for help?*

**Greg Kristan**: My website is having a hard time being found on Google is probably the most common problem I receive. The potential client will list off a few keywords that they want to rank on page one on Google for, but they are currently not there. More times than not, I perform a free SEO audit for the client so I can see if a technical error is present on their website. Most of the time it's a technical error that needs to be corrected to give the website a fighting chance to rank within Google.

*Would you say the technical part is really the foundational part making sure that the website runs properly?*

**Greg Kristan**: Many things can restrict a website's growth. I've seen examples where a business blocked Google from viewing their site, so that is why they don't rank in Google for anything. Before I do keyword research, I always make sure that Google and Bing can view the website without errors.

*What are the most common problems that you see from a technical standpoint that really holds sites back?*

**Greg Kristan**: It varies between websites, but a standard issue is not having proper site architecture. Sometimes a client will have a particular page they want to rank, but there's no clear path for Google bot to get there.

*Do you find a lot of companies are doing what they think they're supposed to be doing? They're creating content, they're trying to do backlinks, but there's these technical problems that render all that work useless?*

**Greg Kristan**: I see cases where people invest a lot of time and money into content creation and design, but the page won't rank in Google. It's frustrating as a business owner when you invest time and money into creating great content, but it's not found by Google. It almost feels like SEO doesn't work and there is no reason to try it again.

*It seems like Google is really making sure that everything is done correct. Do you see that?*

**Greg Kristan**: The web has evolved rapidly in the last few years. Google has high standards for website code, so you have to make sure your site is compliant with their bot. A competitor who is making sure they're technically sound may get the ranking boost over your site if you have a lot of errors.

*I'm sure you've had customers coming to you from other SEO companies that have not been able to find the right fix or produce the results that you can with good technical SEO. Do you see that as a major problem?*

**Greg Kristan**: I have empathy for what business owners are going through when looking for SEO help. They want SEO to help grow their business, but sometimes it does not work out well with their previous SEO company. There are people who promise fast results in SEO, so it confuses business owners when the results never come in. When I start talking about things like a technical review for a client's site, it sounds like an excuse for slow results. I try to ease that concern by sharing as much as I possibly can about SEO to clients. I like to demonstrate that months of no growth led to six straight months of continuous growth for my business, TM Blast. By sharing what I'm doing for my company, I hope that will give a potential client the confidence that I can replicate great results for their business.

*How do you get over the problem with other companies that claim they can get the results in, for example, two weeks?*

**Greg Kristan**: Some ways I try to combat that is to be as vulnerable as I can with my website. I share strategies, things that didn't work, and I share my thought process too. It's important to expose as much as you can about SEO because that can win trust. Being transparent with what does and does not work within SEO allows everyone to be on the same page when a strategy is being initiated.

*Do you try and stay local to helping people in your area?*

**Greg Kristan**: I try to stay local around Massachusetts because I like to meet up with clients. If you are local to the Boston area, I always suggest meeting up to go over your results face to face. However, I do have clients who are not in Massachusetts, so I have regular Skype sessions with them to put a face behind the results.

*Everyone always talks about ranking on Google. You have mentioned Bing a few times. Tell me a little bit more about Bing and the opportunity there.*

**Greg Kristan**: You know, I believe I'm the only SEO person out there that talks about Bing. In the United States for desktop search, Bing makes up over 20% of the search market share. To get more of that traffic share, I use two primary tools to grow traffic within Bing. The first tool I use is Bing Webmaster Tools which is the technical review of how Bing views a website. The second tool I use is called Bing Ads Intelligence. Bing Ads Intelligence will give you keyword data, suggestions, and search volume directly from Bing and

Yahoo. Both tools are free and they will give you a plethora of suggestions specifically to rank better within Bing.

*Is there anything else that stands out as a preconceived notion people have when they're thinking about a search engine optimization?*

**Greg Kristan**: Email spam contributes to the confusion within SEO. Email messages saying I can do SEO for $100 a month while another email says they can do it for $10,000 a month leads to a lot of skepticism. It's hard for a business owner to understand what is credible and what could be seen as snake oil. If somebody comes to you and says they can get you to rank for this keyword in two weeks for $99, it probably is too good to be true.

*Getting back to the technical aspect, what are one or two things that a business can do to help their website rank better?*

**Greg Kristan**: I recommend two tools to help any website rank better via technical SEO. One tool is called Screaming Frog and the other one is called Screaming Frog Log File Analyzer. What's fantastic about both tools is that Screaming Frog shows the technical errors that your website has. When you use Screaming Frog Log File Analyzer, you can see how often Google and Bing come to your site and what pages they crawl and don't crawl. If you combine the two tools together, you can discover problems like orphaned off pages that live on a website.

*Let's talk about some of the clients that you've helped. Is there anyone that sticks out in your mind What kind of problems were they having when they came to you? What were you able to do for them? Ultimately, what was the outcome for their business?*

**Greg Kristan**: I have clients in a variety of different spaces, but the one that stands out is the client who is with the Americans with Disabilities Act. I was excited when he contacted me because I have a friend who builds websites that are ADA compliant. I was able to increase his organic keyword ranks in a few months from technical SEO, so now he is getting more traffic and leads through his business.

*I don't know if you know too much about ADA compliance, but do you know if that will be a big issue for businesses moving forward if they're not compliant?*

**Greg Kristan**: I believe that if you are a business owner, you have to think about the different ways people are going to access your website. Some ways that business owners should think about ADA include things like closed captions in their video, correctly writing ALT tags, and choosing colors that are not hard to distinguish for people who may be color blind.

*Greg, it's been very interesting talking with you. If somebody wants to reach out to you and have you give them a consultation or get an audit of their site, what is the best way for them to do that?*

**Greg Kristan**: They can go to my website directly at www.tmblast.com/. My email address is Greg@tmblast.com. Feel free to send me an email!

# About Greg Kristan

Greg Kristan is the owner of TM Blast where he offers SEO services to small and medium-size businesses. Outside of SEO, he enjoys riding his bicycle around Boston, catching baseball games, and visiting his friends who live throughout the United States.

**EMAIL**
greg@tmblast.com

**PHONE**
877-425-2141

# Kendra "R.E. Fixer" Seck

Kendra Seck is a well-known Mortgage Lender, Realtor, author, speaker and educator in the Atlanta Metro area. She has helped many people turn their homes into an investment vehicle. She is dedicated to helping educate homeowners and investors in the changing Atlanta real estate market how to get access to money to make real estate investing a rewarding endeavor. Her mission and purpose is to empower homeowners to think in a different way about their biggest singular investment. Their home!

# Conversation With Kendra Seck

*Kendra, tell us about yourself and your company and what kind of clients you help in this hot real estate market around Atlanta?*

**Kendra Seck**: You are absolutely right, the real estate market in Atlanta is booming right now. It's definitely a seller's market. A little bit about myself, I've been in the mortgage industry, or banking industry, for 17 years. I've been able to help hundreds of people get into homes, understand financial literacy, build their credit and have better savings and budgets for the future. My niche is teaching clients how to go from believing that a home is only sentimental, to the bigger picture of an investment and something to pass on generational wealth. It is a place for you to build memories, but at the same time, a place for you to be able to start out with a smaller home and elevate to becoming an investor. Instead of being a tenant, you become a landlord, if that makes sense.

*Do people think of it like that or do they just think, "This is my home," and not really about an investment?*

**Kendra Seck**: Initially, many people do think about it like, "This is my home, I have to have shelter, I have to have a place for my family." However, with Atlanta having so many investment shows, many people are becoming more and more interested in real estate investing. They are interested in how they can create their own wealth and real estate is a wonderful way to do that.

*What kind of problems do you see these potential real estate investors run into?*

**Kendra Seck**: We have some really interesting things happen. I always say if you are moving towards a goal and you have a challenge, it becomes a learning experience instead of a problem. I see a lot of investors treating every single home as if they are going to personally live there. Sometimes, they will over-invest in the home. When the goal is for the home to be a rental property, you don't want to invest money for upgrades. I see investors running into issues of just over-spending when they are remodeling or just thinking that, "This is a home I'm going to be in for a really long time." So, their initial investment, they put too much money into buying a home and they're not able to cash flow on the back end of it.

*Ultimately, it comes down to the numbers, correct?*

**Kendra Seck**: Absolutely! I wish you could tell everyone that. I'll have people that want to add a really nice outdoor deck and I ask, "Well what about the properties in your neighborhood? Do they also have decks? Will you do the appraisal on the remodeling that you have done? Will it increase your value?" I'll tell people, "Focus on kitchens and bathrooms. When you walk in a home these things give you the greatest value." I'm always steering my clients to what is going to give them value. Are they going to live in this home? What makes this house a viable investment if they need to sell it or move or because they are building wealth.

*What do they have to think about when it comes to appraisals?*

**Kendra Seck**: An appraisal means that your home is being compared to other neighbors' houses that are up to a mile away from you. So, if you have spent $10,000 putting up a nice deck and no other houses in the community have that, the appraiser may be able to give you two or three extra thousand dollars for that $10,000 deck. It really hasn't helped your value that much because you have spent $10,000 but you are only able to get two or three thousand. You are looking to compare. If your kitchen is outdated and most of the homes in the community have taken down their old cabinets and put in stainless steel appliances, then that is something that you want to do as well so you can be comparable to those other homes and get the most value for the neighborhood.

*First impressions are extremely important. Is staging a part of that when it comes to the selling process?*

**Kendra Seck**: Absolutely. Staging is wonderful. When you walk into an empty home you have to then incorporate a person's vision. And you and I both know not everyone has vision. When you stage the home, you skip that for them. They can see where they would sit the kitchen table and where the couch would go and the room still looks spacious for them and they are able to imagine themselves living there.

*Does staging help sell the home quicker?*

**Kendra Seck**: Absolutely, and it makes the pictures online beautiful. Have you ever gone online to look at a home and you have one picture or two pictures? It's not good. But if you see every room spaced out, where you can put things, it makes a great listing for you.

*There's been a lot of tear downs in the Atlanta area and the building up of new, pricier homes. How do you get an appraisal that will support a new home when the majority of the homes are still the original?*

**Kendra Seck**: That's going back to appraisals up to a mile away. If the neighborhood that the house is in does not have the same plots of homes the appraiser is allowed to go further out. So maybe they can go five miles out and look for the comparables for the home that you built. Other investors are then able to come in and remodel homes, or build new ones, in the neighborhood and use the comparables of your remodel or new construction.

It's good for the community to ride by and see construction happening. Lots of people have more jobs, neighborhoods are looking better and people begin to care more about their homes in the neighborhood and take better care of their curb appeal.

*Since you work with commercial investors as well as residential, let's talk a little bit about the commercial side. What do you do for them?*

**Kendra Seck**: My commercial side is dealing more with hard money. For example, when you talk about homes that have a one story and the investor is going to take the roof off or homes that need a lot of work, many times they can't get conventional financing. We use a commercial hard money, or what is being called soft money loans now, and give them the money to buy the house, give them the money to remodel the home, and give them a regular mortgage until they can refinance out of it or they sell it. That is the commercial side of what I do, where the home is being remodeled or improved for the neighborhood. Many investors are using that type of funding because conventional financing is so difficult to obtain. The interest rates are a little bit higher with hard money, but the products are vast. We have so many products that have emerged within the last three years that are very helpful to investors. I help clients analyze how much their house is going to be worth after they've finished repairs.

*What are some misconceptions that people have about getting a mortgage or hard money?*

**Kendra Seck**: Many times, people will push what they are qualified for. So, when you are on an adjustable rate mortgage and interest rates start going up and you have already pushed your limit, you are then going to be in a payment which you can no longer afford. Ten years ago, we had loans where you didn't have to put that much money down and it was easy for people to walk away from, hence why we had so many foreclosures. I don't think products are coming back now where you don't put any money down unless you are going to live in that home. I'm not seeing investment products at 100% loan right now. I don't know if that's going to come back in the future but I think that's one of the things that harmed us previously. A lot of people are against all ARM loans, adjustable rate mortgages, and I always tell people that education is key. If you educate yourself about a home and you're able to get a slightly lower interest rate, why have a 30-year mortgage if you know you're only going to live in a home for three years? You're going to pay a higher interest rate and you may not need to. Now that the rates are going up, I think adjustable rate mortgages will become more popular. I think mortgages are all about education, what works for you. Everyone doesn't have to have that traditional 30-year mortgage. You can have different tools as long as you're educated and understand those tools.

*There's talk in the news every day about the interest rates going up. What's that going to do for the marketplace?*

**Kendra Seck**: I think it will slow people down buying homes. It's a seller's market even though rates are going up, but I think it will slow people down buying homes and possibly begin our transition over to a buyer's market within the next three years. However, right now we have a shortage of affordable housing, especially in Atlanta and we also have a shortage of quality houses. A lot of people are rehabbing, but not everyone knows what they're doing. With these shortages and people having an interest in being homeowners, I think at some point all of this has to balance out. We'll be able to bring in some more affordable housing, hopefully closer to the city and people will be able to continue to get mortgages at a lower rate. Also, just because interest rates are increasing, they are still at historical lows. A rate at a 5% or 6% is nothing to people who got loans two years ago in the crisis at 9%, right? So, with these rates increasing, I'm hoping people understand they can get less of a home because the payments are going to be just a little bit more with a higher rate but you can still get a home. So, we can keep the housing market viable.

*What is the increase in mortgage rates going to do for investors?*

**Kendra Seck**: I think it's going to do a couple of different things. If rates are increasing, it makes investors mortgages more expensive, so the cash flow on their properties is going to be less than what they were expecting. It will also decrease the number of people that are buying homes from them. Knowing your numbers and being able to get that best rate on mortgages is going to be extremely important for them, so they're going to have to make sure their credit is at a place where they can get the lowest rate while the rates are rising.

*So, what's hot in Atlanta right now? What are the areas that people are moving to?*

**Kendra Seck**: Atlanta is becoming "Hollywood of the South." Popular movies and TV series are being filmed all over Atlanta. Soft Ridge, Doraville, Alpharetta, Buckhead, the Mercedes Benz Stadium are desirable areas. The new Porsche plant is a great area to live around, plus it's accessible to the airport. There's lots of little neighborhoods popping up, neighborhoods that have always been around, but just gentrification's happening as well. So it's very important to make sure that where you're moving will give you that equity and most of inner city Atlanta is doing that for our investors and homeowners.

*What is the construction doing to the demographic of the city?*

**Kendra Seck**: It's changing the demographic of the city, part of it I feel like is necessary and another part of it I feel like is invasive. We have a community that has lived there for years and they have not been able to jointly come together and take care of the community. I think that lets you know there's some things missing like education, like understanding financial literacy, maybe the ability for credit or even government, city, county programs that can come in and help with the remodeling for the current people that live there. One thing that happens when people come in and remodel these homes, they make them triple what the home was worth if not quadruple and the people that are currently living there can no longer afford the neighborhood so we have gentrification. The tax values increase drastically and the next thing you know an entire community has been pushed out and replaced. A part of me feels like people have had enough time to get the community together and they just decided not to, but another part of me absolutely knows that they didn't have the finances or the education or the support of the city to make it a place where they could make it better. I would love to see people come in and take over the neighborhood, absolutely, but I would also like to see a balance of affordable homes where other people who live in the community are able to afford. So let's say if they put in 10 brand-new homes that quadruple what the other homes were, then maybe there's three or four on the next street where some of the original people, especially the elderly, still live and they're still able to have a sense of community.

*There seems to be a lot of people that are choosing to move into the city. Living in the city seems more attractive than ever now. Why do you think there has been such an increase in suburbanites moving back into the city?*

**Kendra Seck**: It cuts down on work travel time, stress, and people are spending more time with their family.

*Kendra, give me a case study of somebody that you've worked with. What kind of help were they coming to you for, how were you able to help them out and what was the outcome for them?*

**Kendra Seck:** Let me tell you about one of my investors. When I first met him, he was a tenant and the crazy part is, he's actually a maintenance manager for an apartment complex for over 20 years. He was given free rent at the apartment complex so he thought he had no need to buy a home. We talked about buying a home and building wealth because his wife was very adamant about wanting to have privacy and so I said to them, go out and look for your first home. Don't worry so much about, 'Is this the best home I ever want to see, I'm going to live here for 30 years.' Just get a home that's inexpensive and can be a great rental property, good rents in the area. They actually listened and bought their first home. They spent $47,000 on their first home. I could not believe they were able to get this REO for that price, but they were. They now rent that home for $1,100 and own four other houses. So, every house that they moved into afterwards, they moved into a second home. The second home is now free and clear so what's happening in the key scenario is they're taking the rent. Even though their rents are about double their mortgage payments right now they're taking the entire payment, paying down their mortgage payment and creating massive equities throughout their household. It's a wonderful thing to be able to see that when you're helping a client, when you give them financial literacy, when you take them from being a tenant to being a landlord, a tenant to a homeowner to a landlord, it's a wonderful thing when they actually listen. They complement the ability for their savings for college for their first child that's going to college. They complement the way that they think about work now. The wife petitioned to work from home. The husband still works at the apartment complex but got permission to sublease the apartment that they give him for free. So he's now getting rent for this sublease that he has no mortgage on in addition to having his primary home and three other properties, a total of four. He has now become a model for his children. He now has generational wealth to leave his children each one of these houses if he wants it, or he can sell them to help pay for college. Or he can just keep them and let equity build. So many options now. When I first met him and his wife I felt like they didn't have that many options. They were just saying, "We need some privacy." The husband was saying, "Well I'm okay, but my wife's not." And the wife was saying, "We really need some privacy to be able to have family dinners to ourselves," things like that. So it's just a great case study to see my tenant go to being a homeowner and go to being an investor.

It's a wonderful thing as far as I'm concerned and I want to make sure that I help many, many more people do the exact same thing. So, it is definitely a goal of mine to help with financial literacy and to help other people be able to go from homeowners to landlords, vice versa or tenants to landlords.

*Well that's a tremendous story. Tell me how people can get in touch with you if they want some help, if they're thinking about buying a property or a first-time home even. How do they get in contact with Kendra Seck?*

**Kendra Seck**: I make it very easy. I always let my clients know if you remember my name then you can get in contact with me. My email address is info@kendraseck.com. I have one phone number, it's my cell phone and I carry it with me to all meetings. That phone number is 770-666-4945 and if anyone wants to look me up or read other information you can just Google my name, Kendra Seck and information will come up about me and contact information. I'm located in Buckhead and I'm very open to making appointments and people coming by the office to meet me as well and continue this financial literacy legacy and moving people from tenants to investors.

# About Kendra "R.E. Fixer" Seck

Kendra Seck is known for her motivation, go-getter-energy, and fearless drive to reach goals both personally and professionally. She excels in identifying what plan of action is needed to create homeowners and real estate investors. Winner of top producer awards and 5-star customer service reviews. She is a federally licensed MORTGAGE LOAN OFFICER and REALTOR.

She has been in the residential mortgage industry since 2000. She has the experience and knowledge of varied mortgage lending products to help clients understand that each of their needs are vastly different. She takes humble responsibility in knowing, most people will be making the biggest financial investment of their lives. She prides herself on offering outstanding service, empathy for all lives situations and quick closings.

Having no regrets in her life, Kendra's a firm believer that everything happens for a reason and that something positive can be found in every situation. Her favorite quote is,

"My goal is not to be better than anyone else, but better than I use to be" - Wayne Dyer.

Kendra has a Masters in Counseling MH Psychology from Argosy University, Eastern Star member and Magna Cum Laude undergraduate from Elizabeth City State University in Elizabeth City, NC. She currently resides in Atlanta, GA with her husband and daughter.

**WEBSITE**

KendraSeck.com

**EMAIL**

info@kendraseck.com

# Implementing a Digital Marketing Campaign That Works

Do you want your business to be seen and heard? Do you need for your prospects to understand exactly what it is you do and why they should choose your company to help them? It's more than just getting traffic to your site. Sure, that is important, but what they do when they get there is more important.

Don Dodds is the managing partner and chief strategist at M16 Marketing in Atlanta, GA. M16 is a top digital marketing agency that specializes in strategy and research, design and development and analytics and marketing. In this interview, Don shares how an individual strategy is most important for businesses to get the best return on investment from their internet marketing dollars.

# Conversation with Don Dodds

*Give us a little bit of background and tell us what got you started as an entrepreneur and marketer.*

**Don Dodds**: My entrepreneurial efforts started when I was a kid probably 13, 14 years old. I had my first car washing business. I saw an opportunity and got a couple of guys to help me organize it. I started to generate some capital and saw that there was real opportunity to build something. I never knew the word entrepreneur, but I liked the feeling of working for myself and helping other people to grow. That got me really excited. Then, I read a book by our current President called the Art of the Deal. That book really fired me up to think big and to achieve big things. I went to college at 16 and after college, I had a really great professor who said I should check out internet marketing. I didn't know anything about it, this was early 90's. So, I started teaching myself HTML and graphic design.

At the time the major browsers were Internet Explorer and Netscape. I started to learn about the differences and how they worked. I started to do some initial consulting and everyone around me said the internet is a fad so I shouldn't focus on it too much. I moved to Atlanta in 1997 and soon got a consulting opportunity with Bell South and I had an opportunity to further hone some basic web design skills. About four years later I sold that company and some eCommerce software I developed. For the next several years I did a lot of business consulting, Microsoft based web development and marketing in the healthcare, medical education and real estate industries.

*When did you start M16 Marketing?*

**Don Dodds:** I saw a big gap where people were not really doing any kind of strategy in the digital growth space. I started to think strategically about what could be done to actually help someone grow a business, so my focus then became building relationships and innovating, and helping businesses grow with a strategic plan in mind. Strategy is the foundation for everything we do. I chose the name M16 because I'm a huge supporter of the military and the M16 is the tactical weapon of choice, but without strategy the tactics are often not very effective. I share the military philosophy that "Proper planning prevents piss poor performance." M16 came together at the end of 2012 and the company was officially launched in January of 2013.

*When did you discover there was a hole in the market and start incorporating SEO in the business?*

**Don Dodds**: Google came to fruition around 1998 and around 2001 I started to digest the idea of what we initially called search engine ranking. By 2006 I was fully engaged with SEO, and started to work on SEO very aggressively. SEO has continued to change in terms of what you need to do to be successful. There was a time where people were doing all kinds of ridiculous things, but now you really need to understand that SEO is an art and science of creating organic value. Content strategy is important, figuring out what your KPIs are and who your target is critical. On page SEO, off page SEO, user experience design, using a mobile first strategy are important aspects of SEO. It doesn't really work effectively without having all the components.

*Before we go into the actual strategy, tell me more about the kinds of clients that you help. Is there one particular area where you concentrate or do you have clients from all different kinds of areas?*

**Don Dodds**: We help clients in many different spaces. We do a lot in the legal space, healthcare, education, financial advisory space and wealth management space. We are literally all over the place. For us, we like the excitement of exploring new areas.

*Tell us about the strategy you have. How does it all work together?*

**Don Dodds**: In order to develop a strategy, we have to first understand the goal. We play in three primary buckets. Strategy and research, design and development, and analytics and marketing. Strategy and research begins with asking the right questions and listening. Listening to the client and really understanding their needs. I think one of the most important steps is what we call our discovery assessment. Clients have the best sense of what their challenges are and will talk about their pain points, you just have to listen to them. Once we understand their needs, we can move into creating a strategy that will allow us to help. We take a lot of time to ask the right questions, listen to the feedback, and then start to formulate a plan about where we need to go. Everything is about smart goals. Goals need to be specific, measurable, attainable, relevant, and timely. Most clients that aren't zoned in on the smart goal concept, say things like, "I want my company to make $20 million this year." It has to be more specific. How are you going to measure that? Is that goal really attainable if you only made a dollar this year? Goals need to be attainable, they need to be relevant, and everything obviously needs to have a time base attached to it. That's how we go about really moving from one place to another. Smart goals are tremendously important.

*Do most businesses have the same pain points, the same problems?*

**Don Dodds:** It's going to depend on the business. The common things we see are no unique value proposition, a poorly developed brand identity and a poor user experience. For example, too many call to actions on a page. If you go to a site and there are five or six calls to action on the homepage, users become confused about where they need to go and what they need to do. Not having enough white space and crowding everything up, and not speaking to the user in language that they really understand, are some of the common problems that we see across the board for all clients.

*What are some of the issues with search metrics or keywords they want to rank for?*

**Don Dodds**: Sometimes the client isn't really sure what their keywords need to be and they go too broad which leads to the incorrect target audience. Keyword research is paramount. You can have the right keywords and throw them on the page, but if they are not positioned properly, if the sizing isn't right, if you're not speaking the right message with the right call to action, none of it is really going to matter. The design, user experience, keyword research, and speaking to the target audience in a way that they understand, is really important.

*Do you find that most companies have a strategy that's just not working?*

**Don Dodds:** Here's some interesting data that I've found. 50% of businesses have no strategy at all and only 13% of those businesses that have a strategy, actually execute it. That is a big problem. We focus on helping companies plan, implement, and execute their strategy. There are specific ways that you can do that. There needs to be specified deliverables. When someone comes to the website, what do you want that experience to be? When most people are looking for information, it's a process. We take them from education to engagement, to earning trust, credibility, and then ultimately ending up with a conversion or sale.

*What does that do for the bottom line once you have a strategy? What kind of difference does that make to the business?*

**Don Dodds**: Generally, across the board we see conversions that are minimum 250% when we employ our engagement strategy. We have lots of case studies where the conversion rate is 800% and in some cases even more. When we think about digital marketing, it's not just the SEO piece. We blend SEO with pay per click, Google Adwords, we do a little bit of social media as well to compliment that. It really depends on what the clients' needs are. Taking digital marketing as a holistic approach is really important.

*You have done a great job of showing up on the map and ranking organically for your own website. How are you able to do that for yourself and your clients?*

**Don Dodds**: Everything comes down to understanding who the target audience is and picking the right keywords and creating the right content. We have keywords that have higher volume and some have lower volume. We pick a mix of both high and low volume keywords to make sure that we have an opportunity to penetrate. Less competitive keywords give an opportunity to really get in and start showing results and building that trust and relationship with the client. Once they start seeing those results, we're able to pull in volume. How we make that happen? Relationship building is important, it sets clients up to be an expert in the space that they are in. If you are in the construction business, you want to be an expert. How are you perceived as an expert? Maybe you need to talk to Neil, right? Talk to you and make sure that the authority piece is in place, but also create the right kinds of blogs, white papers, other documentation, video, all that helps to solidify you as an expert, and you really need to understand who you are and what you're doing, and who your customer is, what they want, and what they need.

*If you're in a competitive market how are you able to rise to the top? How long does it take to get those top spots for a competitive industry?*

**Don Dodds**: Generally, I would say that it takes a year or so of work to solidify dominance. It's not an overnight journey by any means. SEO is a long-term game. It requires patience, it requires diligence and a real understanding of what is changing. Knowing what people are looking for and being able to speak to that, ultimately helping people. It can't just be, let's get some links and throw up some content, it's what are you doing to really help people once they are able to click on your site. If your site ends up not being very good and people can't find any information, it's going to be hard for you to increase your ranking and sustain that.

*What is the most important for ranking? Is it people staying on your site for a length of time, what they're clicking on? What signs does Google look for to say, "Okay, this is the best result that I can show?"*

**Don Dodds**: There are a couple of things. For example, if you typed in responsive web design Atlanta, you'll see a snippet and that actually is highlighted from our responsive web design services page. That snippet comes from having enough content that clearly explains what responsive web design is, and who we are uniquely positioned to be able to do that. That snippet is going to show up. You just have to really understand things like click through rate, conversion rate, bounce rate, exit rate and above all quality content. The algorithm is always interesting to watch and it changes daily. Sometimes the changes are very big, sometimes the changes are very small. When we see those changes, we can see what we call a Google bounce, where you may bounce up one or drop off two. Over time, if you're looking at that and you understand what to look for, then you can sort of stabilize things over a period of time. Sometimes, changing a sentence causes us to go up or causes us to go down. We look at that very carefully. We're able to monitor that and make the necessary changes to show up in a rich snippet like we do.

*What would you say are the best practices for somebody that is trying to get their site up in the search engines for their keywords? What are the most important things for them to be doing?*

**Don Dodds**: Create great content. Register on Google maps is very important, sharing your content with social media, and doing the right kind of research so you position yourself to create the right content. SEMrush is a tool that we use and we highly recommend it. Link building, building relationships is key. If for example, you are looking at Google Analytics, and you're seeing that your bounce rate is really high on a particular page, that means people are leaving that page pretty quickly, they're not finding what they want, they may be going to another page, or maybe discarding your site all together. That kind of affect is going to cause the value of your page to decrease. You need to make sure that content is tweaked to provide relevant information to the user, ultimately that is what Google's after. Google wants to make sure that their users are able to get the best information, the most relevant information for what they're looking for.

*Google is getting better and better at watching out for all those spammy things that might have worked five years ago. Now, you've really got to put up quality. Is that what you're seeing?*

**Don Dodds**: Absolutely, I think quality is very important. I hear people say you need a minimum of 300 words, but they should focus less on the quantity of words and focus more on putting up good quality content.

*What are some of the myths, and misconceptions when it comes to SEO? What do you hear from some clients that are thinking about getting involved with an SEO campaign?*

**Don Dodds**: I hear things like SEO doesn't work. We tried it before, we've hired a company, we spent thousands of dollars, and never saw anything. I think a lot of times, SEO companies aren't doing a good job of helping clients understand what SEO is, how it works, and then providing a regular report so the client can see what's happening with the movement. They need to understand all the things that are being done to make it work. You really have to be committed to make SEO work. It takes time and effort.

*What kind of time?*

**Don Dodds**: Generally, you have lower value keywords and more highly competitive keywords. We take a mesh of both and we explain to the client our strategy. The most important thing clients want to see is progress. When we start a project, we try to get the quick wins right away. If they're on page 10 for example, we're generally able to move them up pretty quickly, within 30 to 45 days, with the less competitive keywords. Overtime, three months or so, they will move closer to page one. Usually in a year, but it just depends on how competitive the keyword is, we can help a client dominate.

*For those companies that are thinking about SEO or they've heard things about SEO and haven't really been convinced, what would say to them? What kind of things do you see that holds them back?*

**Don Dodds**: I think it's not getting results. When people don't get results, they are turned off by the idea of SEO working for them. People need to understand it takes time and can't be done overnight. They have to find the right company who understands SEO and can really help them understand the process.

*You've worked with a lot of the different companies, financial advisors, wealth management, attorneys, medical field, are there any ones that really stick out in your mind that have had great success? Tell me their story, where were they when they came to you? What were you able to do for them? Ultimately, what was the outcome and the bottom line?*

**Don Dodds**: We've got a number of case studies. One in particular, an attorney from New York, has been with us since 2012 before the company started. He was doing his website and SEO himself. He had a couple other guys who were trying to help him. He found me online and we established a really interesting relationship. I told him we had to overhaul his entire website, redo branding, get new content, basically redo everything. One of the changes we made to the website that increased conversions immediately, was the blue submit form button. We changed the button to green and changed the wording to "get divorced." It was a simple change with a huge bottom line impact. Little things like that, increased the business year over year. I think it's up to maybe 800% conversion increase. We've worked with him to bring on other attorneys because the company was growing so much and it's getting ready to expand into another state. Those kinds of success stories are the ones that really speak volumes. Often, we end up developing personal relationships with clients. We ended up doing a lot of business coaching as well. Getting really involved in helping the business itself to grow beyond just the website and beyond SEO itself.

*How can people get in contact with you to inquire about your services?*

**Don Dodds**: The best way is to find me on LinkedIn or call the office at 404-919-6288.

# About Don Dodds

Don Dodds is a Managing Partner at M16 Marketing and an innovative digital marketer and strategist with more than 20 years of experience demonstrating an idiosyncratic combination of creative, technical and business acumen. He is a proven business growth strategist and a multi-award winner delivering unparalleled strategy, web design and digital marketing. He holds numerous Google certifications including search advertising, mobile advertising, video advertising, display advertising and shopping advertising.

As a serial entrepreneur and co-founder of 3 multi-million dollar organizations, he has a keen understanding of how to create and scale a business using digital marketing. Recently, he launched an incubator and marketing innovation hub in Atlanta and is the founder of DMOS, a Digital Marketing Operating System that allows businesses to plan, implement, execute, analyze, report and measure digital growth.

Dodds shares his commitment to supporting entrepreneurs as a speaker, mentor and writer for international online publications like the Huffington Post and numerous syndicated blogs.

A partial list of past and present clients included AT&T, John Deere, the State of Georgia, the Southern Company, Heidelberg, Ross University School of Medicine, Black Book, Travel, Inc., Homrich Berg, Piedmont Park, numerous law firms, financial advisory and wealth management firms, startups and large brands.

**LINKEDIN**
LinkedIn.com/in/DonDodds

**M16 MARKETING**
M16marketing.com

ROSEMARY FRANK, MBA,
CDFA/ADFA, CFE, MAFF

# Financial Crisis
# Creates Confidence

Money seems to be involved in nearly every key event that may significantly change your life. Yet, the emotions that accompany events like death of a loved one, job loss, or divorce, can put you at a disadvantage. Rosemary Frank helps her clients through the financial issues related to these most difficult times. That can make getting through the rest seem a lot easier.

Through it all, Rosemary helps her clients make the best decisions, to deal with the here and now, while keeping an eye on their financial future.

# Conversation with Rosemary Frank
## MBA, CDFA/ADFA, CFE, MAFF

*Tell us about Rosemary Frank Financial, LLC, the clients you work with and the types of situations they find themselves in when they come to you for your help?*

**Rosemary Frank:** I help people work through the financial issues they face while in a life crisis such as loss of a loved one, divorce, or job loss. These are times of great fear, loss and anger, as well as loss of confidence regarding life as they knew it. These are also times that require a different kind of thinking and new financial strategies than previously. Following any one of those events, I continue to provide financial guidance and manage their retirement savings and investments on an ongoing basis.

Of those three situations, clients usually come to me following the death of a loved one or job loss. In the case of divorce, they find me before or during the divorce process for help understanding more about the financial decisions they will need to make in the settlement process. Each of these events require precision focus on the client and what they are experiencing at that time. They are usually unable to focus on the long term without empathy, patience, and understanding. This is somewhat unique in the realm of financial advisory and financial planning. For the most part the industry is a bit archaic and has objectified the client as a target for charts, graphs, and product sales. That is changing, but not fast enough.

I have intentionally and consistently listened to my clients and actually let them shape my practice to what it is today.

The vast majority of my clients are women because we simply connect and our relationship is comfortable for each of us. My focus on death, job loss and divorce is a result of clients' times of greatest needs. It is also a time when they are most able to recognize and appreciate all that I do for them, which is mutually satisfying. Another interesting demographic of my practice is that all my clients are individual clients, meaning I have no couples as clients. Even those clients who are happily married, manage their finances independently and their spouse is not a client. Sometimes a spouse will accompany a client to a meeting, if we need to discuss matters that involve them both, but it just works for them to maintain some financial separateness. And it is more important that I continue to provide my client with what they need than to try to attract the spouse as an additional client.

*How early should an individual start planning for your services?*

**Rosemary Frank:** Death is inevitable. We all know that, but we just don't like to think about it. Sometimes we lose a loved one unexpectedly or, more often, they simply die of old age or an illness associated with old age. Everyone needs to be planning for their own passing, as well as encourage those close to them to do the same. Having an estate plan in place, well organized finances, and a financial professional that your survivors can turn to for information and guidance, can help those who are dealing with emotional loss to focus on their own self-care.

What I see most often is a surviving spouse, usually the wife, who has little or no understanding of the financial situation. For whatever reasons, and there are many, she simply did not fully participate in the financial management of the household. The time to start is now. I once had a woman assure me that she fully understood the family's finances because she paid all the bills. If it wasn't for her, nothing would ever get paid. I said, "Fine. That's all about the money you don't have. Now tell me about the money you do have, like your retirement and investment accounts." She froze, then said, "Well, I have no idea."

With regards to job loss, you should always have an emergency fund in place that will cover at least six months of necessary expenses. Job loss is certainly an emergency. If you can provide for your own financial relief during this time of stress, you will be better able to focus on your job search. Your thinking will be clearer, you will just naturally interview better, and you will be able to truly choose your next career step rather than grasp the first opportunity, which may not necessarily be the best one for you.

There is not too much else you can do before you are suddenly unemployed, but the sooner you call me the better. I once had a fellow call me within the hour of being notified, as he was packing personal items, before he called his wife. I literally walked him through it, until he was in his car, then suggested he call me the next day for an appointment. As a backup to your emergency fund, we should be clear on which additional funds would be used if that becomes necessary and segregate them. Following separation from your employer, you need to rollover retirement funds from the employer plan, review beneficiaries, and pare down your expenses.

Divorce is not something you plan for. But, you can plan to minimize the financial damage to yourself if it should happen. With a divorce rate of about 50% for many years running, you simply cannot deny the possibility that it will happen to you. Your protection is a prenuptial agreement. Not romantic, but it is a precaution. Similarly, while you do not plan to burn your house down, you readily have homeowners insurance. Just in case you need it. A prenuptial agreement will spell out what belongs to whom and who gets what in the event of a divorce. It should be prepared by an attorney, with both parties having legal representation, and well in advance of the marriage with no pressures. I have often consulted on prenups to illustrate long term financial outcomes, for each of the parties, of various scenarios under consideration before the parties agree to the terms. This has helped them feel more comfortable with what they were agreeing to while everyone was in the best of spirits, communication was good and cooperation was excellent. Prenups are not only for the wealthy or celebrities. They are for anyone who cares about what they have, or may have in the future, and realizes the importance of planning as an individual as well as a couple. It will enable you to avoid the possibility of a long protracted and expensive divorce process in exchange for pulling out the pre-nup and getting it over with accordingly.

Given that only about five percent of all marriages are preceded by a prenup, the remaining persons facing divorce need to begin preparing for what is to come as soon as they realize divorce is inevitable. Adequate information and gathering documentation early can save literally thousands of dollars in legal expenses later in the process. Divorce is a legal process, but the issues to be resolved are financial in nature. Even parenting plans, which provide for the care of children, have serious financial ramifications. A significant part of my practice is in helping clients understand their finances, analyze consequences of various property division scenarios, and forecast their future financial condition based on possible alternatives.

The enormity of the financial issues of divorce become evident once a client realizes that it will force every financial decision made during the marriage to be made again. Now, when your emotional stability and reasoning is debilitated. Add to that the likelihood that you may not have fully participated in those decisions in the first place. Add to that the disclaimer that may well be in your attorney's services agreement that they are not responsible for the financial issues of your divorce (although they will spend 90% of the time talking about financial issues). Add to that the hidden tax ramifications, inherent in your settlement, that neither you, nor your spouse, nor your attorney may even know exist, yet one of you will be affected by each of them. Call me as soon as you know this is happening.

Divorce is a time of loss for what might have been, fear of the future, and distrust of a person you thought you knew. I have had a poll on my website for nearly twenty years that asks, "Do you feel confident about your post-divorce financial future?" The results, though not scientific because they include only those who chose to respond, have consistently been 90-91% "No." I help clients become more confident and change "No" to "Yes."

*What do you feel are the biggest myths out there when it comes to personal financial services?*

**Rosemary Frank:** Many people believe financial planning is only for the wealthy. So untrue. Everyone has wealth, or access to wealth, relative to their means, and that needs to be managed. Whatever you have, large or small, more or less, is your wealth. You do not need to be considered "wealthy" to have wealth. There are many financial advisors who would welcome your modest dollars and help you grow your savings and investments. My own minimum is $10,000 per account. If that still seems like a hurdle, then I am willing to help with budgeting and developing good savings habits. No matter what you erroneously think, or how resistant you are, the fact remains that someday, when you no longer have actively earned income, you will need to draw upon savings in order to live. Those savings need to be happening now. If you still don't see it, ask for help.

Procrastination. Some people think they have all the time in the world and will begin to save after they have purchased everything they can think of, moved it to the garage, and ultimately given it away. That day will never come. When it comes to saving and investing, your best ally is time. With time on your side, when you start saving early, your money works for you so you don't have to work for your money. I help you understand how money really works. How much that credit card is really costing you. The power of compound investment returns earnings over many years. I often tell people that spending $100 on a jacket today is like spending $1,000 of their retirement.

The good news and the bad news is that there is a plethora of financial information easily available on the internet, radio, TV, books, etc. This leads many people to believe that financial planning and investing is a do-it-yourself project. That is like reading a biology book and thinking you can take out your own appendix. Information outside your personal area of expertise should be used as a backdrop for working with a professional, asking well informed questions, and better understanding the answers. I would never assume to be able to read a book, or view the antics of a TV "info-entertainer" (whose primary goal is to sell advertising) and attempt to do your job with no professional training. Why would you attempt to do mine? That said, my job is to sift through all the possibilities and make recommendations specific to your situation. The final decisions are always yours to make. I can help you work smarter towards goals you have that remain elusive.

*What are some common misconceptions about personal financial services?*

**Rosemary Frank:** There are many misconceptions about financial planning and the industry is somewhat to blame for that for not having clarity in its structure or processes. However, there are many reputable professionals who are trying to do a better job of communicating one-on-one, one day at a time, myself included.

All financial planners or financial advisors are not alike. First, the two terms are used somewhat interchangeably, but I see a distinction. Financial planning can involve the development of a plan with no specific advice provided regarding implementation of the plan. There are financial planners who do not do securities transactions, nor manage investment accounts. They do not implement their own plans for the client. On the other hand, a financial advisor will provide investment advice and manage investment accounts. In my opinion, it is inherent in the development and determination of that advice that some form of planning would have been necessary. Additionally, an Investment Advisor is bound by the fiduciary duty, which is the highest standard of trust to always act in the best interest of the client. That is always something you should ask about when interviewing financial professionals. My firm is a Registered Investment Adviser *(sic)*, I am a fiduciary and I prefer the title Financial Advisor, although I also do financial planning.

Beyond that, financial planners and advisors can have specialty areas, as indicated by credentials after their name. These specialties will help you decide if they have the expertise that best matches your needs. In my own case, I have a specialty in the finances of divorce, evidenced by Certified Divorce Financial Analyst (CDFA), two other divorce certifications which have since been retired, and Advanced Divorce Financial Analyst (ADFA). My work in divorce, mostly with women, has shaped my client base to be mostly women and individuals rather than couples.

Additionally, a point of differentiations regarding financial advisors is how they manage their accounts. Meaning, do they themselves accept discretionary authority to structure portfolios and make buy/sell decisions in your account, or someone else in their office, or do they use professional portfolio managers? Question the level of expertise they have in-house versus the accessibility of portfolio managers who manage billions of dollars for the largest foundations, pension funds, etc.

Another frequent misunderstanding regarding financial advisors is that they are somehow not to be trusted. We all know what the headlines have been in recent years, but there is good and not-so-good in every profession. Please do not deny yourself the services you need for your own financial well-being because there are a few bad apples. Do your due diligence, check credentials, ask difficult questions. Probe for information regarding the processes involved in managing your accounts for a system of checks and balances. For example, in addition to my own firm registration and regulatory oversight, I process through a separate broker, clear transactions through the largest clearing house in the country, and use professional portfolio managers for daily management of client accounts. That's no less than four separate organizations, working seamlessly and cross-checking each other on a regular basis.

A third misunderstanding is that we will somehow do it all and make it happen. Not exactly true. Some effort will be required on your part. We can provide our best advice, make our best efforts, etc., but you need to give us something to work with. If we say you need to spend less and save more, you cannot counter with why you need to spend that much. Less means less. I won't tell you what you must do without, but something will likely need to change if you want your outcomes to change. Consider the fact that when you earned less, you spent less. Just do "remember when" and go back to that. One of the things I like to do is be sure you "pay yourself first" by putting clients on automated monthly withdrawals from their checking accounts to the investment or retirement accounts. This is the surest way of guaranteeing that regular contributions to accounts are made.

*What are your clients' most common fears about seeing a financial advisor and what can they do to overcome those fears?*

**Rosemary Frank:** One of their greatest fears is that the advisor will be judgmental towards them for not having done better with their personal finances and that they will be made to feel stupid and not understand anything that is said to them. This is so sad. Most advisors recognize that prospective clients are people who have already acknowledge their shortcomings and simply want to do better. Unfortunately, if someone has never met with a financial advisor, their only experience is through the media. I think they can readily discount the power moguls portrayed in the movies as over exaggerations for the sake of drama. What is truly regrettable are the radio and TV personalities who dispense "advice" to the masses and garnish it with criticism, scorn, ridicule, shame and disparaging comments. This leads people to believe that is how they might be regarded one-on-one. What you need to realize is that these personalities are also very much the entertainers and also need to create drama with negativity. If an advisor ever hinted at similar behavior you should leave their office immediately and continue your search for someone with whom you can work comfortably. You can easily get an advance "feel" for an advisor by the tone of their website, viewing any videos they may have available or listening to audio recordings. It can also be meaningful to have a brief phone conversation when you make an appointment, rather than schedule through an assistant. If they are not available for such a conversation, that should tell you something as well.

Another common fear is that engaging a financial advisor will be costly. This need not be the case. First, determine what it is you want to buy. See what they have to offer and how you will benefit. You will have already gotten a valuable financial education just from interviewing possible advisors. When you feel you may have a good match, discuss their fee structure and decide if how you will benefit from their services will be worth it. If someone is able to provide you with a lifetime of financial confidence, how much is that worth to you? If they are available to answer every financial question you may have, on demand, what is that worth to you? Most people are amazed at how little the cost actually is. In my own practice, as a fee-only advisor, I charge a very small annual percentage of invested assets to cover my services as well as those of the brokerage, trading fees, and portfolio manager's fees. For no additional charge, I am available for any questions you may have at any time, whether about your accounts or anything else financial. I want you to call when you have financial questions and not hesitate because of what it might cost for my time. As a fee-only advisor, I am literally invested with you and want you to do well. When your accounts grow, my income goes up; when your accounts decline, my income goes down.

*What other perceived obstacles do you see that might be preventing someone experiencing divorce from using your divorce financial services?*

**Rosemary Frank:** People think they can learn from another person's divorce. Believe me, no two are alike, your friend/sister/cousin/mother probably never fully understood their own that they are now trying to explain to you, and no one is going to really tell you everything. If you are going through a divorce, you have only one chance to get it right. There are no do overs.

If you have been married less than two years, own no real estate, have no retirement accounts or investment accounts, have no children, each of you has nearly equal income (none of which is in stock options, stock, etc.), and neither of you are self-employed, then you can probably get divorced without financial assistance. Anything else, I suggest you begin looking for someone you can work with.

If you think a divorce financial consultant will be too costly, it could cost you more to NOT have a one on your case. About one-half of my current caseload, at this time, involves some form of "clean up" after case went through the process without one. That means you actually paid people to deal with financial issues they did not understand and now you will pay both them and me to attempt to fix it. I first began doing divorce financial work because of the unfortunate outcomes I would see as a financial advisor. I had people come to me thinking they needed a new financial advisor and I had to tell them that what they needed was "a new divorce." Of course, there is no such thing. What they were dealing with was the fallout of uninformed decisions made during the divorce. I knew I wanted to become involved in the divorce process to help with better long-term outcomes. It often takes several years for the potential financial problems to manifest themselves. Other financial professionals see the problems as well. It is not unusual for someone who works in a finance-related profession, like banking, mortgage lending, or insurance, to tell me about the post-divorce devastation they see in their clients' situations. A colleague once told me, "I was taught to never try to save money on parachute packers, neurosurgeons, and divorce financial planners."

When an attorney tells you that you don't need a divorce financial consultant, that should be a red flag for you. They are your authority on the law, not finance. Ask your attorney some difficult questions regarding their financial expertise and how much responsibility they are willing to accept for financial issues in your case and I think the answer will surprise you. If they say something like, "have been doing this for 20 or 30 years and can handle everything," go back to the problem outcomes I previously referenced that I, and others financial professionals, have observed over those years. You are the ultimate decision maker regarding your divorce and I believe your case ought to be managed as you wish, with the professionals you wish. Also, family finances and divorce tax issues have become more complex than ever. The prior days of working 40 years, for the same company, then retire with a gold watch and a pension are gone. Families have, fortunately and unfortunately, been forced into having financial tools and products that they often do not understand and neither do many attorneys. Dividing those assets, and debts, in divorce is even more complex than managing them intact during the marriage.

*When it comes to planning for retirement, what are some of the common pitfalls and mistakes you see people make?*

**Rosemary Frank:** The biggest mistake made by the most people is little or no planning at all. They really have no idea what the future holds for them or how quickly that future will arrive. I often hear things like, "I don't need to save for retirement because I stand to inherit a considerable sum." It is never quite certain how much a "considerable sum" really is. Nor do I probe that issue. No one has any idea what will be left to inherit after the elder lives longer than anticipated and expenditures for health care exceed all prior expectations. We all need to take responsibility for ourselves. The best thing to do is start early, start now, and save sufficiently for you own needs. If you inherit anything, consider it a windfall and be prepared to pass it on.

Another mistake is thinking they need to be ultra conservative with all investments once they retire and begin drawing on them. This either/or "flip a switch" mentality will cause them to lose out on potential continued investment growth opportunities. If you retire in your mid-sixties, you conceivably could live for another thirty years. Therefore, you will not need some of your retirement savings for another twenty to thirty years. With that kind of investment window, for a portion of your holdings, a more aggressive strategy may well be appropriate. Work with your advisor to segment your investments according to when they are needed for everyday living expenses, be diligent and adjust as needed.

Too much thought is usually given to the accumulation stage of retirement savings and too little attention to the disbursement stage. Clearly, the disbursement stage is at least equally as important. Your advisor's job is not done while you are living off your accounts. There are unique strategies to each stage and not all financial professionals are simultaneously attuned to both. It may become necessary to seek out a new advisor to match your needs during the disbursement years.

Sometimes not enough attention is given to taxes and tax strategies. Popular retirement savings vehicles, like the 401(k) and IRA, allow tax deductible contributions and deferred taxation until withdrawal when you are presumably in a lower tax bracket. Upon closer examination, that amounts to planning a lower future standard of living for yourself. In actuality, we do the exact opposite by planning active retirements with travel and social activities. Many retirees found that they were paying higher taxes on retirement account withdrawals than they would have paid when the income was earned. Further, they were paying regular income tax rates on capital gains earned in retirement accounts instead of the much lower capital gains rates paid on non-retirement accounts. This realization led to the creation of the Roth IRA and Roth 401(k) which address some of the problem. In addition, the contribution limits to all of these retirement vehicles, both the traditional and the Roths, do not allow for sufficient retirement savings. The best thing you can do is have the professional help of a financial advisor to develop a multi-prong approach to your lifetime savings and investment needs.

Overlooking the impact of inflation, which is creeping and insidious, is a common mistake. Inflation has averaged about 2.7% over the past twenty-five years. If we assume that may continue, inflation will cause the cost of goods and services to increase nearly 50% over the next ten years, and nearly double over the next twenty. Inflation of health care costs, of more concern to retirees, are at about three times this rate. This totally defies your ability to anticipate how much income you will need during retirement, or how much you need to save now, without professional guidance. Also, try to understand what goes in the calculation of inflation, actually the Consumer Price Index (CPI), to determine what applies to you. What is your personal inflation rate? If you need all the things that are at accelerated inflation rates, like health care, and don't buy much of the things that are decreasing in cost, like electronics, then the CPI does not apply to you. Additionally, we have some politics interfering with a true measure of the CPI from time to time. Specific commodities are sometimes excluded because they are "too volatile" and would be overly impactful upon the Index. Yes, read that again. Is that not what we are trying to measure? For a while, years ago, milk was excluded. That worked so well that now all food is excluded. As is fuel. However, we now have a CPI-E index, calculated for the elderly (over age 62) population and it is consistently higher than the CPI which is widely publicized.

*Can you share examples of how you have helped a client from struggle to success in each of your practice areas?*

**Rosemary Frank:** I have an investment client whom I first met at a seminar where I was presenting. We had chatted briefly and she made an appointment for an initial consult, at which time I came to understand her story. She was in her early 50s, the single mother of a teenager, recent cancer survivor, and had just returned to the workforce. Her savings had been totally depleted due to medical bills and she received no financial support for her child. Her extended family was very limited and friends had scattered as if cancer was contagious. It all seemed a bit dire, but she was eager to start rebuilding. She did have an advanced degree and was able to secure a good employment situation. We discussed her financial goals, timelines, obstacles, her son's aspirations and educational opportunities. We reviewed income and expenses and tweaked a few things to allow for a greater ability to save without compromising too much in the way of lifestyle. She then began rebuilding her financial future one dollar at a time.

Initially, I guided her through some savings strategies in regular bank accounts until she had an emergency fund of at least six months of expenses, then some surplus that would be used to open her first brokerage account. Simultaneously, she contributed to her employer's 401(k) to take full advantage of the matching contribution. Within a couple years she had automatic contributions going into a Roth IRA as well as the individual non-retirement brokerage account and continued with the 401(k). Her accounts grew, and she became even more motivated by her initial financial success. She reactivated an artistic skill which had become somewhat dormant and began generating additional income from it, including writing a relatively profitable book on the subject. Her son has completed both undergraduate and graduate school, on scholarships and work-study, and has since established an attractive career. This story really is as wonderful as it sounds. There were challenges along the way, but I helped her through them. She recently experienced job loss. We have had to slow down her savings rate, but not eliminate it entirely, because she still has long-term goals to meet. I am every bit as optimistic as she is that the next part of her career is being born and we will continue with her financial plan.

I had a divorce client many years ago whom I will never forget for reasons that will become evident. She came to me totally distraught, at which time I confirmed that she was seeing a therapist and she assured me that she was seeing two of them. One was together with her husband, with whom she was trying to reconcile, the other individually. Although he told her he did not want to remain married, he continued this dance of joint therapy and "trial dating." She had moved from the marital home to an impoverished situation. She loved toast but did not have a toaster. I felt like buying her one, but did not want to cross an invisible ethical line. Although she had very little income, and had taken nothing from the marital home, he seemed oblivious to her situation. On one of their dates, he encouraged her to take leftovers and "reheat them in the microwave." She did not have a microwave. She did have a stove with at least two working burners and one pot, so she took the leftovers.

Both parties were self-employed as independent consultants in related fields. She had become dysfunctional and had current income that was a small fraction of his. Their financial situation was blurred by the mixed use of assets and resources, i.e. vehicles, computers, etc., for business as well as personal purposes. They owned their home, but both also officed there. We clarified their respective incomes and post-divorce expenses and developed proposed settlement options for dividing marital property. I pulled it all together, factoring in additional variables like, continued retirement savings, impact of taxes as single individuals, hidden taxes in the real estate, investment and retirement account projected growth rates, future impact of inflation upon income, expenses and purchasing power, and proposed alimony at different levels for differing time frames until she could rehabilitate her business. We met numerous times reviewing what it all meant and provided her attorney with simplified charts he could use in negotiations for a settlement on her behalf. This gave him an advantage over opposing counsel who was merely throwing ideas and counter arguments around with little substantiation.

The process continued to be difficult for her. A lot of tears were shed in my office and she was thinner every time I saw her. It was about eighteen months before they finally settled. Along the way, I had given her substantial documentation that showed what she needed to know and illustrated a dismal financial future with a less than optimal negotiated settlement. I later gave her some supplemental pages and told her to just add them to both her and her attorney's binders. She froze, then said, "I can't." I asked, "Why not?" She said, "I burned them." That was a first for me, and it has never happened again. We had hit rock bottom. I assured her that I understood and promised to prepare another complete set for her. More than a year after that case ended, I had another occasion to work with her attorney, one of the most pre-eminent in the area. He made a point of recalling this case and said, "You know, you did a lot more for her than just crunch the numbers and I want you to know that I really appreciated it. Thank you. And I hear she is doing quite well now." She is. We both see her, from time to time, getting favorable press coverage with advanced thought in her area of expertise, consulting on highly visible projects, and commanding major speaking engagements.

*What led/inspired you to start in your profession, what's your backstory?*

**Rosemary Frank:** I was a genuine case of corporate burnout and wanted to do something much more personal and meaningful. After more than thirty years of doing business research and opportunity analysis, all heavy in finance, I thought the transition to personal finance would be simple. Very few things are ever simple. After I embarked on this new career in personal finance, I was hit with a barrage of study, testing, and licensing requirements that was daunting. I was effectively "back in school" and still had to continue to make a living. At the same time, I was already loving it.

Chronologically, I began in insurance, did some mortgage loan origination, then got my broker's license, then the investment advisory, followed by my first divorce certification. After that, I continued with the brokerage and investment advisory while becoming more committed to the specialty of divorce finance. I was the first in the country to earn three certifications in the finances of divorce, two of which have since been retired, then went on to earn a fourth. To complement my divorce work, I also became a Certified Fraud Examiner and Master Analyst in Financial Forensics. During that time, I was affiliated with two different broker-dealers, learned a lot for which I am grateful, then went independent and registered my own investment advisory firm.

Through it all, I have grown and developed with my clients. They have literally shaped my practice. I listened to what they wanted, how they wanted it, and what I meant to them. It has been extremely rewarding. They determined that my client list would be 90%+ women, most of whom had previously been offended and/or ignored by financial advisors who preferred to talk to their husbands. All I had to do was be there for them. And listen. And understand.

From the very beginning I saw people struggling with the financial fallout of divorce. I knew it did not need to be that way, and wanted to be part of the solution during the divorce, rather than try to pick up the irreparable pieces. Divorce finance is the neurosurgery of personal finance. Everything needs to be cut and divided and you only get one chance to get it right. I don't get to choose what I will know and what I will ignore, as other financial advisors do. They can decide that they will or won't do cash value life insurance, annuities, mutual funds, stocks, real estate investing, private investments, options, college accounts, retirement accounts, trust accounts, precious metals, oil and gas wells, mineral rights, intellectual property and royalties, small business, patents, art and collectibles, etc. I don't get to decide or exclude anything because clients present with what they have and it now needs to be understood, explained and divided in their divorce. They usually don't understand things themselves because they have a cacophony of accounts and financial instruments that were cobbled together over the years with or without professional assistance. To me it's all part of a puzzle. I help people learn and make better decisions.

The formation of my independent advisory firm was a significant undertaking which has enabled me to do more of what I think is best for clients and less of what I see as holding the industry back. All my clients' accounts are actively managed by professional portfolio managers whose only job is to focus on account performance. I use evaluations from an independent research organization to select the managers whom I recommend to clients. There are no deals, no friendships, no quid pro quo obligations. Each manager is recommended based on the soundness of their methodologies as well as actual performance. The management firms are of the highest caliber and responsible for portfolios of tens of billions of dollars each. It is extremely rewarding to be able to offer these resources to my clients.

I am a lifelong learner. My credentialing requires more than 70 hours of continuing education per year and I consistently far exceed that. I also teach continuing education courses to other divorce financial practitioners as well as attorneys. I believe in giving back and have contributed thousands of hours and dollars to professional groups, community groups, and non-profits during the time I have been in financial services. And I will continue to do so.

I appreciate all my clients who have given me not only a livelihood but also a purpose which is continuously renewed and truly amazes me.

*What's the most important thing your clients must be willing to do to become more successful with their personal finances?*

**Rosemary Frank:** Change. Clients must be willing to change.

Different results require different behaviors. Different behaviors require different thinking. Most change is usually difficult, but changes regarding what we do with our money are particularly challenging because attitudes about money are deep rooted and ingrained in our behaviors for reasons we do not even understand. I ask clients to think about their money story: What is their first childhood memory of money? How was money regarded in their family of origin? What does money mean to you? Thinking about money in these terms helps make financial decisions more rational rather than emotional. What we do with money is more emotional than anything else and will continue to be, but we can temper that if we discuss money with some objectivity. The goal is to make financial decisions less of a "rationalization after an emotional decision," and more of a "decision after a rational deliberation." At a personal, internal level, improve your relationship with money and be open to suggestions from your financial change agent, otherwise known as your financial advisor.

Sometimes, other persons in our lives get in the way of our relationship with money. If you are feeling denied of a full relationship with money due to restricted access to it, lack of information regarding household finances, or lack of familiarity with any aspect of how money moves through your family, you may be financially immature. If you have tried to remedy this situation and been denied access to information or full participation in the household finances, you may be a victim of financial abuse which is a form of domestic abuse. Take this seriously and seek professional help to understand why and how this is the case and how to remedy it.

If you have believed that you will never be good with money and avoid doing anything about it because that is just not socially expected, buck the trend. Traditionalists have deemed that there is a profile to people who are qualified to manage money. I don't buy it. It is no secret that 80% of all financial advisors are men, mostly white men. They seem to have been born knowing how to fix cars and manage money. If you don't believe it, why might you continue to act as if you do? It has actually been proven many times, through research, that women consistently experience better investment performance results than men. Then there are the "first borns" who are perceived to have gotten more brain cells than any other child, male or female, who follow. Then there are the tall men who far outnumber short men as CEOs. Society's ideas of who is smarter, or seems more capable, screws up our heads. I encourage you to question all this nonsense and summon up the power to do better for better results for yourself. "Power" and "control" are both good words to improve our thinking, behaviors and outcomes. I'm talking about "power to…" do something, not "power over…" someone. And "control to…" do something, not "control over…" someone. Nor should you ever be the "someone."

It is remarkable that, considering we live in a world of constant change, we remain so resistant to change when it is about consciously changing ourselves. Get over it. You are constantly changing whether you want to or not. The best we can do is direct that change in ways that are beneficial to us. Be open to new information on topics, like finances, that may seem frightening, distressful, terrifying. Ask questions. It is my job to answer your questions and help you, not judge and intimidate you. And believe me, nothing shocks me anymore.

*What are your final thoughts on the topic of personal finance that can help someone be more successful?*

**Rosemary Frank:** Success is so relative and depends upon what you want. Therein lies the more difficult work of determining exactly what it is you want. What are your priorities? With your personal finances, does a well-funded retirement take priority over next summer's vacation? If you say, "Yes," then you need to act as if it's true, skip the vacation, and fund your retirement. That will be your success. If you say, "Not really," or "I want to go anyway," then go and have a successful vacation. But you will have a less successful retirement.

Realize that everyone has financial fears, whether they admit it or not. Women worry about becoming bag ladies. Men fear being ostracized if they don't get the next promotion and raise. Both define themselves by what they do rather than who they are. No wonder they don't know what they want. So, how will they measure success? Just realizing the problem is much of the solution. What keeps you up at night? Let's talk about it. I cannot be your therapist, but I do know how to talk about money.

That brings up an interesting point. I work professionally with a lot of therapists, have them present at divorce workshops I do every month, and sponsor some of their professional events. There seems to be widespread consensus that therapists do not talk about money. The CEO of a national psychotherapists professional organization told me they discuss that avoidance all the time and even dislike asking for their own fees. Patients have neglected to pay them for sessions and they never asked for it. Wait, money is the number one cause of divorce, and the therapists are not discussing money? I feel like my two worlds have collided.

By default, you make financial decisions every day and this series of decisions essentially becomes your "plan." Whether intentional or not. Like the saying goes, "If you fail to plan, you plan to fail." I would wish better for you. Financial planning is not rocket science. It just takes a bit of self-discipline and assistance from someone who understands how money really works and can explain it for your benefit.

If you are facing divorce, I hope you realize that it is now just really about the money. I dare say that 90% of the discussion with your attorney will be about money, yet they are not a financial professional, nor do they want that responsibility. Get yourself some specialized divorce financial assistance, bring clarity to the situation, expedite the process with facts rather than uninformed conjecture, assure full disclosure of all assets and debts, and make your points with convincing evidence.

Personal finance is exactly that. It's personal. It's in you to learn. It's in you to know better. It's in you to do better. Personally, I'd like to help you do that.

*If someone feels they want to plan for retirement, so they can feel confident about their financial future, how can they connect with you and what will happen when they do?*

**Rosemary Frank:** I'm easy to reach and invite all inquiries. Visit my website, RosemaryFrank.com and click on "Contact," call 615-595-6850, or email me directly at Rosemary@RosemaryFrank.com. We will have a brief conversation, when you can tell me what prompted you to reach out for help, so I can determine if an initial consult would be beneficial to you. I may ask you to bring specific financial documents with you, but I will not ask you to complete any tedious forms. I will simply want to learn as much about you, and your financial goals, as possible during that meeting. Forms will come later. We will schedule a one-hour meeting for the initial consult, which can be telephonic or in person.

During our meeting, I will answer all your questions to the best of my ability, explain my processes as they apply to your needs, show you a sample investment proposal or consulting report, as appropriate, and remain as transparent as possible concerning myself, my background and how I work for you. I charge my regular fee, $225 per hour, for the initial consult. If you indicate that you would like to become a financial planning or financial advisory client, that fee may be waived. If you become a divorce financial consulting client, that fee will come out of the retainer you provide. All major credit cards are accepted.

When you decide to use my services, we will work out a schedule of next steps together in a way that allows you to be comfortable with the pace as well as the process. Subsequently, you will find that I am consistently available, dedicated to serving you, will respond to all contacts promptly and/or initiate contact regularly. I recall one particular client, whose account set-up process was very complex, requiring steady contact for several months. When it was all completed, she was nearly alarmed by the absence of things to do and said, "Oh my gosh, so when will I see you again?" I assured her that I would remain a constant in her life and now see or talk with her at least once every 3-4 months.

# About Rosemary Frank, MBA, CDFA/ADFA, CFE, MAFF

Rosemary Frank is Principal of Rosemary Frank Financial, LLC, a fee-only Registered Investment Adviser. She provides services in wealth management, divorce financial consulting, and other attorney support services. Bound by the fiduciary standard, she always puts the client's best interests ahead of all other considerations.

Her wealth management services are dedicated to helping individuals understand how money really works. A large part of her practice is focused on meeting the needs of women in all stages of life, but particularly following divorce, death of a loved one, or job loss.

As a divorce financial consultant, Rosemary has worked on hundreds of divorce cases providing litigation support, expert witness testimony, or financial neutral services. She has emerged as one of the foremost divorce financial practitioners in the country and is considered a thought leader at a national level.

Previously, Rosemary held corporate management positions where she completed extensive business research and opportunity evaluations, including mergers and acquisitions, for publicly traded firms. She prepared critical presentations for investor audiences, as well as business outlook content for Securities and Exchange Commission (SEC) filings and Annual Reports.

Rosemary received her B.S. degree from Rochester Institute of Technology and her MBA from the University at Buffalo, SUNY. She is a Certified Divorce Financial Analyst (CDFA), Advanced Divorce Financial Analyst (ADFA), Certified Fraud Examiner (CFE) and Master Analyst in Financial Forensics (MAFF). She is also a TN State Supreme Court Listed Rule 31 Family Law Mediator, specially trained in domestic violence. She has authored numerous Continuing Legal Education (CLE) courses, on the financial issues of divorce, and taught nearly two hundred CLE classes. Rosemary previously held active General Securities licenses, and a General Securities Principal (supervisory) license, before transitioning to the fee-only advisory service model. She is also an Arbitrator for the Financial Industry Regulatory Authority (FINRA).

**EMAIL**
Rosemary@RosemaryFrank.com

**WEBSITE**
RosemaryFrank.com

**LINKEDIN**
LinkedIn.com/in/RosemaryFrank

**OFFICE**
615-595-6850

**CELL**
615-497-1856

**FAX**
615-250-2724

# Your Own Magic Pill

Randy Gonigam is a sleep expert, speaker, and the Founder and President of Essential Bed. Randy has helped thousands of people achieve their desired sleep outcomes over the last 40 years.

Everything Randy does, from sourcing and design of their beds, to their unorthodox channels of distribution, to the stripping of all unnecessary costs from their business model in order to keep prices low, is designed to recognize, understand, and solve the serious problems and threats their customers face to their physical, mental, and emotional health. All three are intricately tied to the quality of sleep we get.

# Conversation with Randy Gonigam

*Tell us about Essential Bed, the clients you work with and the types of situations they find themselves in when they come to you for your help?*

**Randy Gonigam:** We are all looking for that one magic solution. The supplement industry is a multi-billion-dollar industry and growing. We see advertisements every day for diet pills and products, creams to make our skin look younger, products to boost our energy and increase our muscle mass. We consume energy drinks (another multi-billion-dollar industry). We read endless books on focus and creativity, diet, fitness and relationships. In short, we are on a constant search for the key to a better life.

What if I were to tell you that there truly is a supplement that does all of these things and much, much, more? This supplement has been extensively studied and reviewed by some of the leading academics and universities and has been conclusively shown to have zero negative side effects! New benefits of this supplement are being discovered on a regular basis. Here is a brief outline of what this supplement is already known to do:

1. It makes the skin look younger
2. It helps us lose weight and keep it off
3. It gives us higher energy levels
4. It makes us smarter
5. It makes us more attractive
6. It helps us build muscle and get the most benefits from exercise

7.  It improves our memory
8.  It enhances our focus
9.  It helps combat depression
10. It increases our feelings of happiness and well being
11. It helps us to have better relationships
12. It makes us more effective and productive at work
13. It improves our reaction times and decision making abilities
14. It enhances athletic performance
15. It helps prevent nearly every disease and illness from the common cold to cancer
16. It promotes healing

That's a pretty impressive list and it's only a partial list. And every single claim made has been clinically proven in an abundance of clinical studies to be absolutely true.

Here's the catch: you MUST take this supplement once a day as prescribed to reap the benefits. Failure to do so may, in fact, have serious consequences.

So, if I could give you this supplement, with these benefits, and all you had to do was to take the daily dose as prescribed, would you be interested? Think it's too good to be true?

Well this magic supplement not only exists, it is readily available to all of us.

This supplement is SLEEP.

Sleep is a passion that has become my life's work. As someone who has personally struggled with sleep issues, I have an empathy with the struggle of others. I am fascinated by the science of sleep and the amazing way our bodies and brains are wired, with sleep as the facilitator for all our physical, mental, and emotional processes. It seems like literally every week, scientists are discovering another way that sleep impacts our lives.

And yet, most of us do not seem to put a high enough value on sleep. We give up precious sleep hours to any number of other activities, then self-medicate with caffeine and other stimulants as compensation. We say, and even believe, that we don't need sleep, that we'll sleep when we die. The reality is, that lack of sleep IS killing us, and the ever-growing tidal wave of rising health care costs is directly related to our sleep deficit and the consequences of that deficit.

There are many factors that go into quality sleep. There is an entire tool chest of "hacks" to help us sleep better, including total darkness, white noise, temperature regulation, nutrition, exercise, etc. Our habits go a long way toward determining our sleep. For most of us, quality sleep is under our control with a commitment to these habits.

We (my team and I), have chosen to focus on one of the most important tools for quality sleep: the bed. My professional journey has led me to my purpose which is to help as many people as I possibly can find better sleep (and all the positive benefits that accrue there) by collaborating with them to find the right bed for their individual needs. We feel like we are changing lives for the better, one good night's sleep at a time.

In our business, we meet and assist a wide variety of people from all walks of life. What they typically have in common is a dissatisfaction with their present bed, and a trepidation they feel as they are looking for a new one. Finding and purchasing a new bed can (unfortunately) be an intimidating and often unpleasant experience. Entering the "mattress store minefield" of hard sell salespeople, bait and switch advertising, and convoluted, even blatantly false claims of benefits and performance is not generally a pleasant experience.

At Essential Bed, we meet our customers in a very relaxed, laid back atmosphere. We do little advertising, as most people come to us via either word of mouth referrals from their friends and family, or professional referrals from the doctors and other health professional we work with.

It sounds overly simplistic, but we try to interact with all our customers in a relaxed manner, and that generally enables them to share with us their needs and issues revolving around sleep. It's important to recognize that your bed is one of, if not the #1 touchpoint in your life, and sleep is the single most important thing you will do to promote your own physical, mental, and emotional wellness and health.

Without quality sleep, it is literally impossible to lead your best life. And while most people, especially when they are younger, take sleep for granted, it is a nightmare (pun intended) when suddenly confronted with sleep issues that are robbing your quality of life.

So, we find ourselves intimately involved with strangers, helping them to solve sometimes very challenging and complex issues. We take this responsibility very, very seriously and that requires a much different type of experience than the customer is going to get at a mattress store, furniture store, etc. Our approach is very diagnostic. We take the time to really find out about the customer's total needs, and we often uncover additional issues and needs that the customer did not even realize are related to their sleep.

A large part of this approach is to educate our customers as to the myriad ways that sleep affects their lives. We try to provide our customers with a toolbox for getting their best possible sleep. Our greatest tool is the bed, and of course that is where we can provide the greatest benefits to our customers. But we also expose them to other tools they can use to get even better, healthier sleep, and it is very satisfying to be able to help people in this way.

Another commonality among our customers is that in probably 90% of the customers we work with, one or both people (if it's a couple) have pain issues that make it difficult to sleep and that are having a significant quality of life impact. One of the reasons we have intentionally partnered with Chiropractic Physicians and Physical Therapists is that we can often provide substantial pain relief. Most mattress providers really do not understand these issues, and we are constantly undoing damage that resulted from a store, or even a medical professional guiding that customer to a bed solution that made their problems worse, not better.

So our customers come to us with a variety of critical needs, and our diagnostic approach can really make a huge difference in their lives.

*How early should a family start thinking about their sleep needs?*

**Randy Gonigam:** You know, this is such an important topic, and for us, one of our greatest frustrations. Candidly, very few people really think aggressively about the sleep needs of their children, and about how those sleep outcomes may impact their lives and long term health.

Kids are programmed by evolution to sleep 18 plus hours a day as babies, gradually coming down to typically 9 to ten hours a night as teens. The baby part is pretty cut and dried, as what parent doesn't want their baby to sleep as much as possible? But once they are past that baby stage, things often get pretty murky.

There is the issue of sleep quantity, as well as sleep quality. And families have issues today that just weren't there in past generations, specifically the addiction to screens of all types. So, parents need to approach the issue of sleep for their kids in a very intentional manner, and from a very early age.

So, ask a basic question.... does the way we approach sleep quality really make much sense? First, we take human bodies that are all kinds of shapes and sizes, featuring arms, legs, stomachs, hips, shoulders and lay them flat! The body is not flat. On top of that, we typically lay that (not flat) body on pretty firm, even hard surfaces. And then, as these constantly developing young bodies move from 18 hours nightly to 12 hours, then 10 hours, then less...we completely disregard that gravity, an undeniable and unchangeable force, is relentlessly pressing these (non-flat) bodies onto these flat, hard surfaces. Now factor in 18 years of this cumulative force, and you begin to see where some lifelong issues may begin to develop.

And it gets worse.... Quite often, we have our children sleeping on extremely low quality, often hand me down mattresses. So, I want you to think about the hand me down aspect: your child, in that person's most vulnerable and formative life stages, is breathing in, night after night, the dead skin cells, allergens, pathogens and bacteria of whoever used that mattress previously! Yuck, gross and OMG. And depending on the situation, possibly pet dander as well. Mattresses tend to become either the #1 or #2 source of dust mites in your home (carpets being the other main source), as dust mites feed on the dead skin that we all slough off in the night. If safeguards haven't been taken, your child may be inhaling years and years of accumulated dust mites (dead and alive) with every breath.

And now the screens. There are a couple of very good reasons to carefully control your child's usage of screens in their bedroom. Many studies point to serious sleep disruption caused by exposure to the blue light present in cell phone, tablet, computer and TV screens, when those screens have been used in a 1 hour proximity to going to sleep. Not to mention the legions of teens that sleep with their devices, waking up dozens of times a night to notifications, texts, etc. Several studies have suggested a link between brain cancer and sleeping with our phones near our heads. GET THE SCREENS OUT OF THE BEDROOM!

Numerous studies have confirmed that the greatest thing you can do for your child's grades, their emotional health, their physical health, and literally every aspect of their lives, is to instill quality sleep habits and continue to reinforce those habits throughout their childhood, adolescence and teens. This is truly the greatest gift you can give your kids.

We are not suggesting that you have to break the bank and place your kids on expensive, state of the art sleep systems (although this would be a much wiser investment in their long-term health and happiness than virtually any other). But we do suggest at least this...No hand me downs when it comes to mattresses. Don't get them a bed that is too hard - they need pressure relief on their shoulders and hips (just like you do!) and a hard bed will NOT support their developing skeletal systems. They don't weigh the same as adults, and thus their comfort and support needs are different as well. And as they grow, if at all possible, move them out of that twin bed and up in size.

As we noted earlier, sleep and your bed are the biggest touch points in your life, and this is even more true in the lives of your kids. No one's life was ever improved by a lack of sleep.

*What do you feel are the biggest myths out there when it comes to choosing a mattress?*

**Randy Gonigam:** Without question, when it comes to choosing a new mattress, more people make a mistake and choose the wrong mattress due to **the myth of the extra firm bed.**

There is so much confusion and misunderstanding of this topic, that it is always one of the very first topics we cover with a customer. It seems like so many sources of information get this wrong, from mattress salespeople to doctors and other professionals. We have found many mattress manufacturers that don't understand it. And yet, it's quite simple:

**COMFORT AND SUPPORT ARE NOT THE SAME THING.** It's perfectly appropriate to talk about extra firm support. It is nearly always a mistake to let that same extra firm terminology come in to the comfort conversation.

This is where it is important to note that we are all different, although we all have some things in common as well. And everyone feels "firmness" differently. It is not unusual for a couple to be trying different beds and completely disagree as to which one is "harder." Neither one is right or wrong, they just perceive things differently, much the way people can disagree on a color, with some insisting the color is gray, while others being equally adamant that it is blue!

So here is how we approach this topic with our customers: they can rely on us to only show them beds and solutions that have the best support - we only offer premium support beds. That support may be arrived at by a number of different technologies, but it will always be up to the task. The most important part of the process, is tailoring the comfort of the mattress to the individual sleeper. Because no matter how great the support is, you are just not going to get your best rest if you aren't comfortable. It seems obvious, but in reality it trips up many, many people.

Why is this such a big problem? I would venture to guess that over half the customers I meet for the first time tell me "I need a firm bed because I have a bad back." Reality: some of your back issues may be directly related to sleeping on a bed that is too hard.

Let's go back to what we said about kids' mattresses, gravity and the human body. If you are laying your (not flat) body on a hard surface, and then subjecting yourself to 7 to 8 hours a night of gravity relentlessly crushing your body onto that surface, you are extremely likely to develop some pain issues. Picture your body...in all likelihood you are wider in the hips and shoulders. Now see yourself laying on your side on a firm bed (it's easiest to get a mental picture of yourself this way, but the principle is the same for back sleepers). Your body's weight is now being mostly supported by your shoulders and your hips.

When the bed's surface is too firm, you are literally bridging your torso between your hips and shoulders, causing your spine to sag. Your shoulders and hips sit higher with your torso sagging between. And our friend gravity never stops. It ceaselessly smashes your weight straight down via your shoulders and hips. Eventually, we see several problems. 1) Rapid and constant buildup of pressure points on your shoulders, arms and hips, causing you to squirm, move, and toss and turn - interrupting your sleep. 2) Breakdown of shoulders and hips resulting in pain, and 3) Back pain due to lack of adequate, continuous support of the torso.

To compensate, sometimes we become "tummy" sleepers. Now your hips and shoulders are really sitting higher and your back sags even more. Bad choice. Don't be a tummy sleeper!

A bed that allows your shoulders and hips to drop far enough to be cradled with corresponding reduction in pressure points will allow your torso to be supported and kept in alignment with your shoulders and hips. It is at that point the support comes into play, taking the work of the comfort layers and holding your body in this aligned position.

For flatbed sleepers, quality specialty foams do the very best job of getting your body into the most stressless and supportive position. However, remember what we said at the outset - if you aren't comfortable, you will never get the quality sleep you need. From experience, we know that about 1 in 3 people just don't like sleeping on a foam bed. It's foolish to try to overcome that issue. We have innerspring beds that come extremely close to performing like a specialty foam bed, and we have hybrids that combine the two technologies.

Remember, **comfort is king when it comes to your new bed.** The biggest mistake by far that people make is confusing comfort and support, therefore purchasing a bed that is too hard.

Finally, the whole myth that we are best served by sleeping flat. In our opinion, the most positive trend we have seen in sleep health is that more and more people are choosing beds with adjustable bases. These beds allow you to raise and lower both the head and foot of your bed, and can be absolutely life changing to reduce stress and pain in your body.

I've literally seen tears from people when they sleep pain free on an adjustable bed. I just wish people would start earlier (in their 20's) rather than later in life when gravity and flat sleeping may have already inflicted so much damage. And for all you mothers out there: imagine the advantages of an adjustable bed during pregnancy and after!

*What are some common misconceptions about sleep, mattresses and the mattress industry?*

**Randy Gonigam:** The biggest, and by far the most dangerous misconception people have about sleep, is that they don't need that much of it. And that is a key reason why we have higher health costs than any other country in the world.

Fact: our bodies are wired by evolution and genetics to get specific quantities and quality of sleep. And if you do not get that sleep, you have at least a 25% greater chance of dying in the next 10 years.

Fact: there is nothing in your life that is improved by inadequate sleep. We push ourselves to work longer hours, sacrificing sleep to get more done, when the reality is quite different. Working less hours and getting quality sleep nearly always results in greater productivity. We drive fatigued, which closely resembles, and is just as dangerous as, driving drunk.

Our relationships suffer from poor sleep. Our brains fail to filter harmful comments that hurt the ones we love. Anger simmers close to the surface. We cannot process interactions in healthy ways. Depression builds on itself. The list of harm caused by poor sleep is endless. You can find much more about the tragic consequences of poor sleep at EssentialBed.com.

Another of the common misconceptions is just the expectations people typically have of a mattress. Unless there is a specific problem such as pain, tossing and turning, heat, etc., people tend to never give their bed a thought, even though they spend ⅓ of their entire life there!

It's not unusual for people to express disappointment or anger that their 10 or 15-year-old bed needs to be replaced. They don't think about the fact that after 10 years they have literally spent 3 years of their lives laying in "their spot" on their bed! Of course, it is no longer performing like it was when it was new.

The fact is, for the use it gets, and the benefits it provides, your bed, regardless of cost, will provide you with more value than any other purchase you make in your life. And that's the truth.

There is a misconception that certain name brands are superior or can be trusted just because they are well known names. After all my years of experience, I have developed relationships and have hands on experience with virtually every well-known brand name in the industry. And frankly, for various reasons, I do not typically recommend any of them.

I have spent years researching and working with various mattress brands and technologies. My interest is in being able to offer the best solutions for our customers at the best value (pricing) possible without sacrificing quality and performance. And I believe wholeheartedly that that combination of performance and value is rarely going to be best from the best-known brands.

There are several lesser known bed builders and innovators that share our commitment to sleep health. These companies use breakthrough technology to continuously innovate and improve. And many of these can create genuine greater value, as they are privately held and not answering to Wall Street's constant need for profits at the expense of all other considerations.

Another misconception is that you can get a quality bed for an incredibly cheap price. Now I understand that everyone may have a different view of what cheap is, and everyone has real budget necessities that have to be adhered to.

But the mattress industry in general, and mattress store chains most egregiously, have relied for so long on false advertisements of price savings, as well as bait and switch advertising that frankly, I don't know why anyone would believe their claims. Look, no one is selling mattresses for half off or more of their real value (with the possible exception of the occasional soiled, floor model closeout). When you see beds that are 50% off and blah, blah, blah, you can be certain that those beds were never sold at the higher price. The 50% off price is the price it was always intended to be sold for, and is extremely profitable to the seller. Don't believe the nonsense.

The fact is that you are going to have to pay a certain amount to get a bed that can even approximately meet your needs. If your budget will not allow you to get a bed that meets at least your minimum needs, you are probably better off with a short-term solution such as a quality camping air mattress.

Another misconception is that specialty foam beds sleep hot. While there is definitely truth to that thought, particularly in the past or with low quality product, today's specialty foam beds that are carefully engineered and built with quality components, are now made to dissipate heat and keep it away from your body during sleep. We are happy to say that we have not encountered a heat issue with any of our customers in years that was related to the bed itself, as we are extremely conscious of this potential issue.

The reality is that any trapped heat issues we face today are always traced to the sheets or bed protector/mattress pad the customer is using. Wildly exaggerated thread counts on modestly to cheaply priced sheets create a sleep environment that doesn't breathe, trapping body heat above the sheets where it builds on itself and leaves the sleeper in a puddle of their own sweat. If your body heat cannot pass through your sheets and to the bed itself, the bed cannot dissipate that heat.

*What are your clients' most common fears about sleep and purchasing a new bed?*

**Randy Gonigam:** A mattress purchase is a relatively big ticket purchase that will be used for, on average, eight to ten years. It is not easy financially to rectify a mistake. And it can be miserable to sleep on a mistake for eight to ten years, not to mention the debilitating effects poor sleep may have on your health.

This is why we are so committed to a diagnostic approach to helping people choose a mattress. By spending a little extra time with customers, asking the right questions, really listening to the answers, and gently guiding them through the process, we nearly always get their bed choice right the first time. Because we are committed to their sleep quality first, and because we see the bed as the most important tool to quality sleep, we stay away from just selling the most popular bed, or our personal favorite or whatever. Instead, we focus in on the customer's actual needs, and it makes a huge difference.

Most mattress retailers today, including us, also offer a sleep trial period, so if a mistake is made it can be rectified without catastrophic financial consequences to the customer.

*What should people do to get past those fears?*

**Randy Gonigam:** Simply put: participate in the process with us. Open up and tell us about issues you have related to sleep. Tell us about what keeps you awake. Let us in, so that we can truly help you get to the best solutions to improve your sleep. Be open to the broader chest of sleep tools.

We've helped thousands of people to improve their lives, enhance their health and relationships, and just plain be happier through quality sleep. Trust us to help you, as well.

*What other perceived obstacles do you see that might be preventing folks from having success with sleep?*

**Randy Gonigam:** I need to reiterate this point: It is IMPOSSIBLE to live your best life without quality sleep. We must learn to value sleep above all, because it is the regulator of our lives. Here's what I mean:

Sleep time is when the body regulates hormones. Without proper hormonal balances, things go haywire pretty quick. Want to lose and control your weight? Sleep better. Want to reduce your chances of heart disease, diabetes, stroke? Sleep better. Your #1 hedge against cancer? Sleep better.

Lessen the chances of dementia? Sleep better. Get better results at the gym? Sleep better. Have a better marriage? Sleep better. Have better relationships with family, friends, co-workers? Sleep better.

Want to be more attractive? Sleep better. Want to be smarter? Sleep better. Want to be better and more successful in your career? Sleep better. Want to live longer? Sleep better. Want to improve your quality of life? Sleep better.

And yet, Americans often do not value sleep. We exchange sleep to binge watch TV. We trade sleep hours for social hours and partying. We mindlessly surf the internet when we should be sleeping. We throw out statements like "I only sleep 4 hours a night and it doesn't bother me" (wrong). "I'll sleep when I'm dead." (True. Just likely to be sooner rather than later).

The truth is it is a very small fraction of the population (less than 3%) that can function properly long term on less that 6 hours of sleep a night. Chances are, you aren't one of them.

We talk a lot with our customers about the Health and Fitness Triangle. Two sides of the triangle are exercise and nutrition, while the base (foundation) of the triangle is sleep. People seem to have a great awareness of the exercise and nutrition aspects, but often give little thought to sleep. And yet, without quality sleep the actual positive effects of good nutrition and exercise are severely limited.

If you have tried and tried to diet and control your weight with limited success, or if you have not seen the results you are seeking from your exercise efforts, it may be that you just are not getting enough quality sleep for your body to maximize your efforts. So much of your results are tied to hormonal balance, and sleep is the regulator of these hormones. Insulin, cortisol, gherelin, leptin, adrenaline, and all other hormones are intrinsically tied to sleep.

And yet it seems like sleep is often the first thing to be compromised when prioritizing our time. People don't think twice about giving up sleep to binge watch TV shows or movies. We go out socially until very late at night, not only sacrificing crucial sleep time, but often enjoying alcoholic beverages that are proven to interfere with sleep quality. We will hang out on social media or text with friends well into our required sleep hours, creating a sleep deficit that will undoubtedly negatively impact our lives at some point.

No one wants a home without a good foundation. It is foolish to live life without some degree of thought and planning. We make financial decisions with care. But sleep, the very foundation of all health, wellness, and quality living, is scarcely thought seriously about or planned for. But I guarantee that your sleep habits will have a profound effect on your life.

*How can these pitfalls or mistakes be avoided?*

**Randy Gonigam:** Like anything else in our lives, good habits are likely to yield good results. For sleep, those habits are simple to develop when you recognize the importance of sleep to your overall health:

1.  Keep consistent hours for sleep and waking up. For reasons we do not yet fully understand, our most valuable sleep time seems to be between 10pm and 2am. Try to go to bed at a consistent time that maximizes these hours

2. Eliminate caffeine after 2pm. Caffeine's effects have a half-life of four hours. You are still experiencing some effect after eight hours. Limit those effects by stopping intake early.

3. Eat your evening meal three to four hours before retiring. If you must snack, make that snack fresh fruit or vegetables, or just a small amount of lean protein. Avoid any kind of processed foods in the evening.

4. Cut off your screen time at least one hour before retiring. Read a book, meditate, do puzzles. If you read on a tablet or your phone, get and use an app that cuts out the blue light.

5. Have sex. Sex is great for getting you ready for sleep.

6. Keep your bedroom completely dark. Even the slightest light can interrupt sleep activity.

7. Have a source of white noise in your bedroom. Every home has little noises. The white noise will cancel them out.

8. Keep your bedroom cool. 64-68 degrees is optimal for sleep.

9. Limit your liquid intake in the evening to cut down on those bathroom trips,

10. Learn your personal sleep cycles and time your wake up to coincide with the end of a cycle. You will feel much more refreshed and energized.

Sleep deprivation is so widespread in our society that it is truly a public health crisis. How many tragedies could have been averted if sleep deprivation were not involved? Many of those that we trust to keep us safe, including law enforcement personnel, doctors and nurses are often chronically sleep deprived while making literal life and death decisions.

The NTSB states that over 100,000 automobile accidents a year have sleep deprivation as a key cause. An estimated 6000 or more fatalities are linked to lack of sleep. Nearly 40% of drivers in one study acknowledged falling asleep at the wheel for at least an instant!

Develop good sleep habits. Instill those habits in your spouse and in your children. Avoid needless pain and suffering. Sleep!

*How have you helped someone get better sleep?*

**Randy Gonigam:** One customer with whom we eventually developed a close friendship came to us with a particularly challenging set of circumstances: she was experiencing back, shoulder, and hip pain that caused her to wake up frequently to reposition. She suffered from chronic acid reflex that was especially active when she slept. She had experienced some tough breaks and was really battling with depression. And she was struggling financially.

We addressed her problems in a series of steps. After asking her some questions, it became clear that the bed she was currently sleeping on was far too firm for her, and was a major contributor to her pain and repositioning issues. Being sensitive to her limited finances, we got her on a relatively inexpensive, but very high quality foam mattress, with the understanding that she was sacrificing some level of durability in order to get the pressure relief she needed at a price she could handle.

The mattress brought a level of immediate relief that was literally life changing. As she stayed in her sleep cycles longer, and experienced significantly more REM sleep, she woke up more refreshed and energetic, and her depression receded significantly. We helped her find extensions for her bed frame to elevate the head of the bed, which helped to minimize the symptoms of her acid reflex. And we talked about sleep habits, and she changed her current behaviors to align with her sleep goals.

The results for her were nothing short of euphoric. The change in her quality of life was just incredible. Not perfect yet, but compared to where she started, she felt like she was experiencing a miracle.

Eventually her life circumstances and finances improved and she upgraded to an even more sophisticated mattress and added an adjustable base. Now she gets even greater pressure point reduction and can utilize sleep positioning to relieve and release stress on her body. Her acid reflex is virtually a thing of the past due to a focus on proper eating habits as well as sleep positioning. Her energy levels are off the charts and she has begun swimming and playing tennis!

The bed, as a tool, played a major part in her success story. But her commitment to sleep and developing great sleep habits also played just as big of a role. And we are so proud to have a part in this story.

It's not difficult for you to have the same type of experience. It starts with a choice...a decision to value sleep and to develop the habits that will almost certainly pay dividends for a lifetime.

*What inspired you to help people with their sleep?*

**Randy Gonigam:** Like a lot of folks, I kind of stumbled into my life's work, which then became my passion, and finally my calling. Young, aimless, but full of dreams, I found myself working in a retail furniture store to pay some bills. And despite having never given one thought in my life to retail, sales, or the furniture and mattress industry, I absolutely fell in love with all of it. I couldn't learn enough, and I sought out every success story in the industry to ask questions and learn more.

My wife and I worked extremely hard and created a couple of really terrific stores, where we satisfied thousands of customers and provided real value to our customers, and to our employees. We raised two amazing daughters who now have wonderful families of their own. Unfortunately, we had to close our business during the Great Recession, and at that point in my life I had to discover what was truly important to me in terms of career.

Long story, shortened, I eventually realized that my long-held passion for providing my customers with the best beds possible at the best prices possible, was actually the jumping off point for following my calling. The more I learned about sleep, and the more I saw the breakthroughs in sleep science taking place today, the more I knew what was going to be the next chapter in my life.

It is important to my wife and I to give real value, and to help people wherever we can. Our mattress business truly offers life changing benefits to our customers, and we are proud to serve them in a personal, authentic way.

*What's the most important thing folks should consider to become successful with their sleep?*

**Randy Gonigam:** Sleep may be the most important factor determining the quality of our health, the very quality of our lives. The importance of quality sleep cannot be overstated. The entire health profession is really waking up (pun intended) to the critical role that sleep plays in every health process. And not just physical health, but mental and emotional health as well.

I would recommend to everyone that they take an active role in their personal sleep health as soon as possible. The sooner you start sleeping your best, the faster the benefits of that sleep will accrue. Don't wait for health issues to find you...be proactive and put your best preventative defenses in place now, for a long, happy, healthy life.

*Any final thoughts you'd like to share, and how can you be reached?*

**Randy Gonigam:** It's your body, your health, and your life. There is no "perfect bed solution" that is correct for everyone. Don't be swayed by advertising or an aggressive salesperson into buying a bed that does not fit your specific needs.

Your bed and your sleep will be two of the most valuable touchpoints in your life. Don't settle. Get the bed (tool) that helps you get the best sleep, and open up the "sleep toolbox" and form the habits that will enable you to get your best sleep for your best life.

We are here for you. There is a ton of great information at our website EssentialBed.com. My personal email is **Randy@EssentialBed.com**, where I am available to discuss your sleep needs. If you live in Northern Illinois, visit our showroom in North Aurora and let us give you the personal attention you deserve to find the right solutions for you.

If you don't live in Northern Illinois, don't worry. We can ship anywhere in the U.S. and our diagnostic system can help you by phone or email. We are really good at this, and we will make sure you get the right bed, **guaranteed**, wherever you live.

Drop me an email, or call us at (630)-592-8602 to talk about your sleep needs. Remember, sleep is the perfect supplement, with endless benefits and zero negative side effects. And all of those benefits are available to you, without a prescription, as long as you follow the directions, and always take your daily dose!

# About Randy Gonigam
## Sleep Specialist
## President & Founder, Essential Bed

Randy Gonigam has a 40-year background in the retail Sleep Industry. His passion for providing quality sleep solutions began in his early twenties and has never abated. He has helped thousands of people to achieve their desired sleep outcomes. He has been featured in media throughout the world and speaks frequently about sleep health and the consequences of lost sleep.

Always seeking the best answers and innovations, Randy and his business team bring their life changing sleep solutions to their clients through a variety of alternative channels including serving patients of a wide-ranging group of Chiropractic physicians and other health professionals, personal trainers, physical therapists and their retail stores. Their diagnostic methods to helping their customers achieve quality sleep have also raised hundreds of thousands of dollars for non-profit organizations with their highly successful Fundraising Mattress sales.

Randy and his wife of 38 years live in a quiet Midwestern town and enjoy watching and experiencing their daughters, son-in-laws, and five grandchildren as their lives unfold.

**Email**
Randy@EssentialBed.com

**WEBSITE**
EssentialBed.com

**FACEBOOK**
Facebook.com/EssentialBed

**OFFICE**
630-592-8602

**CELL**
815-378-5189

# Product Development Coach

Ron Golembieski's inventor and product development coach story started in the St. Pete/Clearwater Florida International Airport. The airport was crowded with passengers, including Ron waiting for our flight that had been delayed for five hours. All the seats were taken, and every outlet was too. Having to charge his phone, Ron went searching for an outlet. The only ones Ron could find were in the middle of the wide-open walls, with nothing around to set his phone on, so it went on the floor. That disgusting floor. But Ron sat on the floor, with his phone so it didn't get stepped on.

Fast forward a few weeks, Ron was watching TV and a commercial comes on, set in an airport, showing phones on the floor and all over each other near an outlet. This brought Ron right back to Clearwater and knowing that he would be in that situation again at some point, Ron jumped right on Google and started looking for a way to keep his phone off the floor in that situation. There was nothing.

So, with the thought fresh in Ron's head, he went into his garage at 11:30 pm, found an outlet cover, a few mini hinges, and some scrap plexi-glass and within an hour, he had his first prototype and "The Pocket Shelf "was born!

Over the next two years, Ron was able to turn his vision into an actual patented product and take delivery of his own inventory. In mid-2017, Ron was asked by HSN to compete with about 100 other new innovative products for the combined HSN and Good Housekeeping Magazine's search for the next recipient of the Good Housekeeping Seal of Approval.

Although he was not selected as a finalist, HSN was so impressed with The Pocket Shelf, they offered Ron a segment on "American Dreams", this is where HSN highlights entrepreneurs with cool new products during Prime Time on their show. This has been an amazing journey and Ron enjoys sharing his story and what he learned with other aspiring inventors.

# Conversation with Ron Golembieski

*Ron, tell us about PRsF innovations L.L.C. and how you are helping first-time product developers.*

**Ron Golembieski:** PRsF Innovations is my first company and my first business. What I learned while putting together not only a company but a business, while also moving a vision, an idea, from my head through the Patent process and into production, is that there are a lot of small intricate pieces and parts that all have to go together, in the right order at the right time. It took me a very long time to figure this out. I help others that are just starting out, navigate this daunting task. There is a lot of help out there, if you know where to look.

*What is one big problem you specialize in solving for your clients?*

**Ron Golembieski:** Taking an idea from your mind to an actual product, is a very long and involved process, especially if you're going to seek a Patent. Through hundreds of hours of my own research, going through the Patent process myself, filing provisional patent applications, and currently working on filing a design patent application, I have learned where resources are, to help people quickly move through this process. Some people say that business is a battlefield, actually getting to that business part however, is a minefield, I want help people take days, weeks, months, and even years off of their process.

*What type of outcome can our readers expect to enjoy by working with you?*

**Ron Golembieski:** I will provide you with all the resources and information that you need to get started, and direction to help you work through your process, saving you time and money and so you can do other things, and business along faster.

*Describe the difference achieving this outcome can make in their life.*

**Ron Golembieski:** The information that I provide took me hundreds and hundreds of hours to compile. Although this information was and still is freely available, you have to know where to look. Figuring out where to look takes a lot of time. I provide you with direct links to the information that you need to make well informed decisions about your business. Potentially saving you hundreds of hours, and lots of money. A very simple and concise punch list of how to move ever forward, and the steps, in order, to take to get you there efficiently is an invaluable tool to save you time and money.

*What do you feel are the biggest myths out there when it comes to developing brand new products?*

**Ron Golembieski:** I think the biggest myth out there when it comes to developing brand new products and having the next great idea, is that you have an idea, and in a couple of days or a month, you're selling product and making your fortunate. I'm not sure if Mark Cuban was the first one to say this, but he's the one that I heard it from, as he said, "It took me 10 years to become an overnight success." Business as a whole moves incredibly slow. Just prepare yourself for that inevitability, what you would expect to take a week could take a month.

Another myth is if you make the better mousetrap, everyone is going to want it. The reality is, getting the decision makers to either take your call or return your call is next to impossible. What you have to understand is these people get pitched hundreds of "better mousetraps" every single week, they have everyone and their brother trying to find ways to get around their people to get directly to them via phone call, e-mail, or any other way that they can think of, they are approached in lobbies, in airports, in bathrooms, and even when they're out to dinner with their families, so to standout and actually get their attention is incredibly difficult.

But it can be done, persistence, respect for the person and their space, and research can land you in their presence, when that happens, you need to be prepared, respectful, and direct to the point. The elevator pitch got its name a from the idea that you get onto an elevator with the one person that can change your life or change business and you will have until the elevator doors open, and they get off, to sell them on your product, or your idea, or yourself, generally it's 30 seconds to 1 minute, make sure you have your pitch ready. It's much more difficult than it sounds.

*What are some common misconceptions around the Home Innovations Industry?*

**Ron Golembieski:** I think the biggest misconception is that if you have a great idea for home improvement or great new product that it will sell itself, nothing could be further from the truth. To get your products seen, you have to market it properly, and proper marketing is very, very expensive. You can try to do it yourself, but you will end up spending a lot of time to make very little progress. Having a great idea for new product, getting a patent, getting it into production and having inventory, that's the easy part. The real work starts when you market and sell it.

*What are some of the most common fears about bringing new product ideas to the market?*

**Ron Golembieski:** A lot of people are afraid that developing a new product from scratch and getting it to the production phase is just beyond their ability. I think this is a very common fear, there's a big fear of the unknown and some people think that it's big businesses and companies that invent things, when in fact most things that you see on the shelves, started out as an idea in someone's head, just like you. Bringing a product to market isn't really about your ability, it's about your passion. If you don't have the passion, you will not succeed, it's really that simple.

Another fear is failure. What if it doesn't work? The cold reality of innovation is that over 98% of all new products never see the shelves, this goes back to having passion. Bringing a new product to market is so difficult that if you don't have the passion and you're doing this strictly for money or fame you probably won't succeed. But, if you have the passion, your passion will lead you to putting in the work that required to making sure your innovation succeeds, it is not easy, do not be fooled. The time, effort and energy that you put into your new products will be a directly reflected in your success, or lack thereof.

Then there's worrying about what everyone else is going to think about what they are doing. This is a big one as well, we as a society tend to gauge ourselves on what other people think. And people in general including family can be very condescending when you say you have "invented" something. I don't like the word inventor because of this, I prefer the words "product developer." Obviously, they both have the same meaning, but sometimes it seems if you say you're an inventor, people look at you like you have four heads. You need to be very good at explaining exactly what your product is, what it does and how it works, and how they would benefit from it.

Some even worry about liability and personal risk. At the end of the day, if there's no personal risk there's no reward. The personal risk that you're going to layout is very real, this risk is not just financial, it is also time taken away from your family, taken away from holidays, weekends, and vacations, but at some point, you have to jump. To have the support of your immediate family your spouse, your kids, is incredibly important, they have to be on board.

Your goal, in chasing your dream, and taking all of this personal risk, is too have the ability to provide a much better, brighter future for everyone. They all must understand, as do you, that this will not happen overnight. Steve Harvey's book "Jump" is a great book to read to find some motivation. In his book, he talks about how at some point you have to jump, and when you jump you have to realize that your parachute may not open right away, you're going to hit the cliffs, you're going to bounce off the walls a few times, you're going to get bruised and battered and beaten up, but, if you believe, and you work hard, your parachute will open.

*How can they get past these fears?*

**Ron Golembieski:** I don't know if you'll ever get past the fear, I truly believe that everyone from startups, to product innovators with new ideas, to the top executives of the top companies in the World, all have fear. What makes the difference, is how you manage it. The best thing that you can do for yourself, is to do your due diligence, make sure your idea, your product is something that people want and can use. In the very beginning, this can be difficult until you get some protections. I wouldn't put too much at risk until you can prove to yourself, and to strangers, that your widget is something special and the public will want it. After you prove that, then it's just managing fear. One way to manage fear is to understand that fear and excitement are the same exact emotion. Everything physically that happens to you in a moment of fear, nervous twitching, heart racing, sweating, etc., Are the same exact physical traits that happen when you get excited. It's all in how you look at it, if you believe that it's fear, that it's fear. But if you believe that everything that's happening to you, is a result of excitement, then you'll get excited even more. Allow yourself to have that paradigm shift.

*What other perceived obstacles do you see that might be preventing first-time innovators from seeking the help of a Product Development Coach?*

**Ron Golembieski:** Being a product innovator is very atypical for most people. Most people work a W2 job and they don't know that its people just like them, that innovate and make the products that we use every day. Sometimes people believe that you have to have some certain, super-secret, high tech degree, to be called a product innovator, this thought alone, I think, prevents many people from at least trying, to get the idea out of their head.

*Should cost be considered an obstacle?*

**Ron Golembieski:** There are many, many are resources that are absolutely free, most larger cities have Think Tanks, Tech Gardens, Makers Spaces, and just about a everywhere hands a SCORE chapter. SCORE, stands for Service Core Of Retired Executives, when you contact them, they will set up with a retired executive, in the exact field that you need help with, for free. There certainly will be cost involved, but in the beginning, you can do most of this for free, up to the point that you are sure that you have a winning idea, and you need to jump.

*What about protecting their idea?*

**Ron Golembieski:** Being afraid to share your idea should be a very real fear. You have to be careful when you share your ideas outside of those that you trust, until you have IP protection, anyone can swipe your idea and make it their own and there is nothing that you can do about it. When it comes to sharing your idea with someone from SCORE or a product development coach, there are certain protections that you can put into place, an NDA is a good start, having a well thought out, and filed, PPA is even better.

The fear of being ridiculed or laughed at, by your family and friends, because you're an "inventor", is also very real, and can prevent a lot of people from wanting to share their idea with those that they trust, seeking their input and their opinions, to gauge if their idea is worth acting on.

*What are some of the little-known pitfalls or common mistakes a first-time product developer can make?*

**Ron Golembieski:** They have an idea and they do not do their due diligence and run to one of those companies that you see on TV, that will take your great idea into production immediately. Do not do this. The next one, is doing your due diligence, you need to do more than just a quick google search to see if your idea is already out there. You should spend the better part of the week if not longer doing research, chances are, your idea has already been done and patented. If you don't do your due diligence you're potentially wasting a lot of time and a lot of money.

*How can these mistakes be avoided?*

**Ron Golembieski:** When you do your research, you actually WANT to find your widget, you want to find the EXACT thing that you thought of. Does that sound crazy? It really isn't, and I'll tell you why. If you're doing your research and you don't want find what you're looking for, chances are, you're not going to find it. While you're doing your due diligence, if you want to find what you're looking for, and you do everything in your power, to find exactly what it is that you're looking for, and after exhausting every possible avenue that you can think of, you still can't find it, chances are it's not out there. And that's a good thing, a very good thing. After you've done your due diligence and you didn't find anything now's the time to really hone down your idea and refine it.

Make the very best drawings that you can, write a great Detailed Description (DO NOT get overly detailed here, if you list a measurement, a color, an exact feature, etc., THIS is what your product will be held to, nothing more, nothing less, these are EXACT documents, don't paint yourself into a corner with your words!) and file a PPA. After that is done you should go seek out SCORE, they can help you move forward from here.

*What inspired you to become a Product Development Coach?*

**Ron Golembieski:** I spent hours and hours figuring out every part of this, every piece of this puzzle, as I went along, at some points, it's so incredibly frustrating that I would spend days working out an issue, and in the end when I finally figured it out, I realize it's something that should have taken me 10 minutes, but I wasted days. These are not just wasted days, and wasted hours, these are hours and days that I've taken away from my family and taken away for myself. If I can help someone move toward their goals, and save them hours, days, weeks, even months, just by sharing what I've learned, that would be incredibly fulfilling to me.

I believe everyone has an idea in their head, most people are afraid to share their idea in fear of being labeled a crazy inventor. So many people have shared stories with me that they have an idea, but they have no idea on what to do with it or where to start. I have heard many stories of people that have an idea and take it right to one of the TV advertiser shows, and are told that they have nothing. That may be true, but, what new product innovators don't understand, is that we are in the rejection business.

Just because one person doesn't see your vision, doesn't mean you should call it quits, and when they reach out to these places that are supposed to be the authorities' because they are on TV, and they are told that they don't have anything, they take that as gospel truth, and they quit their journey before it even started. I want people to understand that every single product that they see, that they use, was invented by someone.

A machine, a computer or a program didn't just think of this idea, of this widget, and then it magically appeared on store shelves, that's not how it works. Someone, somewhere, had a light bulb moment in their head, and they chased their dream. What I want to do is to show people that through simple steps, they can start this journey on their own, in their own home, not relying on someone else who doesn't see their vision; that they can bring their idea out of their head into the market.

*Can you share a lesson you learned early on, that still impacts how you do business today?*

**Ron Golembieski:** When you first start, the amount of effort and energy that you put into creating your business is directly reflected in how fast your business wheels will turn. You have to be willing to commit yourself to your business and making it grow every single day. When you take hours off, take days off, and take weeks off, your business stops almost immediately. When you put the effort and you see the return. This is a constant. Until your business has a team and you can delegate projects off your plate, you will not be able to rest. You will, in some form or fashion, be directly involved every single day, for hours each day.

*What was the biggest mistake you made?*

**Ron Golembieski:** My biggest mistake was thinking that getting through the Patent process, into production and having inventory, were going to be the hard parts. I thought, as soon as I have inventory, I could sell them, and they would fly off the shelves, no problem. Boy, was I wrong. Marketing is a huge part of your business and this should be addressed in the very beginning stages of your business.

*And what were some of the obstacles and misconceptions you had to overcome?*

**Ron Golembieski:** The obstacles that I had to overcome were enormous, because I knew absolutely nothing about starting a business or how to bring a product from my mind to actual production and Patenting. The misconception is that; if you have a great idea, everything else is gravy, this is tremendously misleading.

*What's the most important question first-time innovators should ask themselves as they consider taking an idea from napkin sketch to retail?*

**Ron Golembieski:** Without question, the most important question that you should ask yourself and consider this- do you have the time to do this, do you have the passion to do this? If you're not passionate about what you're doing, you will not go very far. This takes so much time away from your life, if you're not passionate about it, you will give up.

*What's the most important thing first-time innovators should consider when evaluating a product development coach?*

**Ron Golembieski:** There are many parts and pieces that go into developing a product. I think you should evaluate a product development coach based on the coaching that you need, this may be product design, patenting, marketing, prototyping, etc. Having said that, there are plenty of product development coaches that can bring you through the whole process. They typically have product development companies, and with these companies, you need to be very careful. You need to do your due diligence and research them up, down, sideways, and backwards. Most of these companies are stand up companies, however there are plenty of companies out there that will rip you off.

Generally, with any type of product development company or coach, there are fees involved, they are usually significant. However, the more work you do on your end, the less they have to do, the less expensive it will be for you. So, if you bring a product development company an idea, on a piece of paper, a napkin sketch, and you want them to develop it out, refine it etc., they're going charge you much more than if you bring them a product that you already have a Patent on or you're in the prototype stages of. If you need them to get you to production, in that case they may not charge you anything, outside of the costs of the molds etc., just expecting that you're going to go through them to manufacture your product. There's a million different ways to make deals, you have to make the deal that's best for you.

*How can someone find out more about Ronald Golembieski and PRsF Innovations L.L.C. and how you can help?*

**Ron Golembieski:** You can go to my website ThePocketShelf.com,

Or my Facebook page Facebook.com/Product-Conception-through-Production-Marketing-Napkin-sketch-to-retail-1346016368785800/ or email me directly at info@thepocketshelf.com

# About Ron Golembieski

Ron Golembieski is an accomplished inventor, former Marine and Syracuse New York Fire Fighter who works with other inventors and product innovators to help them reach their product goals faster and easier than they could do on their own. Ron's company PRsF Innovations is the parent company of his patented Pocket Shelf; a multi-purpose, collapsible, self-adhering, portable shelf unit.

Ron's development journey with the Pocket Shelf took him all the way from napkin sketch, to prototype, to patent, to production model, to selling online via his business website, ebay, and Amazon. Ron even won an appearance on the Home Shopping Network. Ron learned a great deal through lengthy and sometimes expensive trial and error as he made this journey.

Ron knows what it is liked to face adversity on the path to new product development and how lonely it can be at times. That is why he is excited to share his lessons learned and provide advice and encouragement to other inventors/entrepreneurs as a product development coach.

**WEBSITE**
ThePocketShelf.com

**EMAIL**
info@thepocketshelf.com

**FACEBOOK**
Facebook.com/Product-Conception-through-Production-Marketing-Napkin-sketch-to-retail-1346016368785800/

# Digital Marketing Expert

Living Sky Marketing started about two years ago. In 2016, Robert was looking to invest in a business that could really help people so he figured what better way than to help local businesses grow their own business. He decided to invest in a local marketing agency.

# Conversation with Robert Kerr

*Tell us about Living Sky Marketing, Ltd. and how you are helping your Clients.*

**Robert Kerr**: We help local businesses with all aspects of their online presence starting with foundational things. By making sure all of their directories and listings are accurate by fixing NAP (Name, Address, Phone number) errors. We also help them with review generation by soliciting their clients via email and custom postcards to generate reviews.

We also have done for you Social Media aspect where we have live digital agents posting up to four times per week to Facebook, Twitter, Google + and LinkedIn. We also monitor the web 24/7 to make sure our clients reputation is always top notch.

*Describe at least one big problem you specialize in solving.*

**Robert Kerr**: One of the biggest problems we solve is with a business' on line presence. We first do some research to take a snapshot of how they are perceived on line by people who are searching for them and it grades them on their listings, directories, review and social media and then we work with them to improve on each area.

*Describe the outcome that can be achieved working with you.*

**Robert Kerr**: The outcome that our clients get is measurable results when it comes to their online presence. When we get everything fixed online, Google sees that hundreds of places online as well having he exact same information and this results give them much higher relevancy scores, when people are searching for their product or service.

The difference this can make in their business can be huge. If you can go from not being found in search results to being found.

*What are the advantages of generating leads for business owners?*

**Robert Kerr**: I guess you would say that generating new leads for your business is the lifeline of all businesses if you're not generating new business soon you will be out of business. The advantage of creating new leads on a consistent basis helps a business owner sleep at night.

*What do you feel are the biggest myths out there when it comes to business owners generating leads for their business?*

**Robert Kerr**: I think one of the biggest myths about online lead generation for small and medium-sized businesses is that the cost will be out of reach, but the fact of the matter is it is the most cost effective way to advertise because of the ability to target your ideal clients and not waste money targeting the general public with traditional advertising such as TV, radio and print.

*What are some common misconceptions around the Digital Marketing Industry?*

**Robert Kerr: Digital marketing is only for large business**. Nothing could be further from the truth. Digital marketing is for all sizes of business.

**I don't need digital marketing**. Digital marketing is like the company's online door to their business to welcome them in and to service them. For many it may be the only chance to get their product or service in front of the right people.

*What are some of the most common fears about generating leads for their business?*

**Robert Kerr**: Beyond their ability? There are many different things that can be done online to fit in most any business budget.

What if it doesn't work? One of the best things about digital marketing is we as marketers are able to provide measurable results to our clients unlike traditional marketing. We can show how many times their ad was shown or how many people have been directed to their website or landing page.

Can there be damaging side effects? I guess if you do any kind of marketing improperly it can have a damaging side effect. With what we are able to do in the most cost-effective way is create brand awareness to keep our customers top of mind when people are looking to purchase what our clients are providing.

Personal Risk? Some may perceive that there is a personal risk, but the reality is it can be very risky for a business do no nothing, no customer – no business.

*How can they get past these fears?*

**Robert Kerr**: They can get past these fears by working with a good marketing consultant that has their best interests in mind that can put together a good step-by-step plan that will help them meet their business goals and objectives.

*What other perceived obstacles do you see that might be preventing business owners from seeking the help of a marketing consultant?*

**Robert Kerr**: I think the perceived obstacles for business owners hiring a marketing consultant is who do I hire? We sit down with clients and find out about where their business is now and where they would like to get to. We will put together some recommendations and if they think we are a fit, we go from there. Another obstacle is of course, will it cost too much? When we put the recommendations together it is always in a tiered approach so that we can do what needs to be done, it is in stages to make things both more affordable and effective.

Yet another obstacle may be how much time will it take? The time it takes can vary, but any online market campaign should be given a minimum of three months.

*What are some of the little-known pitfalls or common mistakes you see business owners make on the road to generating leads for their business?*

**Robert Kerr**: Well, there's a few. One of the biggest pitfalls is trying to do online lead generation themselves which takes time away from what they are good at in driving their business forward. I compare it to a painting project that I undertook at my own home. When I was finished, all I could see was all my mistakes. I'm hiring someone to do it next time. They may also just boost posts on Facebook. It's easy, but not very effective compared to what you can do with all the targeting that Facebook has built in to get your perfect target audience.

*How can these pitfalls/mistakes be avoided?*

**Robert Kerr**: These pitfalls can be avoided by working with a marketing consultant to put together a very focused marketing plan to make sure your message is in front of the right people at the right time.

*Can you share an example of how you have helped your Clients overcome these obstacles and succeed in Generating Leads for their business?*

**Robert Kerr**: We have a local restaurant here in Saskatoon that we supplied a Mobile App; Through good marketing from their management and staff, they were able to get over 2,000 customers to download their app. Now on a weekly basis, they send out a push notification with weekly specials at the push of a button. They have said it has been the best and most cost-effective advertising they that have done.

With a local RV dealer, we were able to utilize a system that allows us to capture the ID's on phones of people that were shopping at all the other RV dealers in the local area. Once we capture them we are able to show ads to them in real time, but we are also able to retarget them after they leave and shown our client's marketing message on all of their devices (phone, laptop, tablets and even their work computer) In three months we were able to show their ad (impressions) 471,003 times with 871 people clicking on their ad and going to their website. Again, these people were actively shopping for what our client is selling.

*What inspired you to become a Marketing Consultant?*

**Robert Kerr**: I have always been interested in marketing and have been involved with several local businesses over the years and I always found that trying to figure out the best way to get the right message in front of the right people (buyers) was always a challenge, but also a great opportunity.

When I started to look at today's landscape I realized that marketing was moving more and more away from traditional methods (TV, radio, print) and to where all the eyeballs are moving to and that is online (digital). So, it inspired me to learn all that I can about the digital space, and believe me, I continue to learn more on a daily basis to best serve my clients.

It was a couple or three years ago that I saw a webinar on what a mobile app could do for a local business or organization or even a school that really peaked my interest for local marketing. Since that time I decided to invest in a local marketing agency that can provide a variety of different solutions since no two businesses are alike. What drives me is the difference I can make to my client's short-term and long-term success. I am currently working with a chiropractor in Arizona that is really struggling. We are just starting to work together, but he knows if he doesn't start doing something online he will be out of business. It is knowing that I can the difference in the outcome a business that really drives me to help as many local businesses that I can.

*What's the most important question Business Owners should ask themselves as they consider generating leads for their business?*

**Robert Kerr**: The most important questions a business owner needs to ask himself before undertaking lead generation is "Where am I now and where do I want to be." They need to know where they currently are as far as customers and how many more customers it will take to reach their goals. Once they determine that, then they can talk to different marketing consultants in both online and offline methods to determine what is the best route for them to take. It may be a combination of both.

*What's the most important thing Business Owners should consider when evaluating a Marketing Consultant?*

**Robert Kerr**: I think the most important thing to consider when considering a marketing consultant is the trust factor. When sitting down with them, do they care about me or are they just trying to make to sale to benefit themselves? I like to consider our business as a trust-based business. Our mission is first and foremost to be a fit for our client's business needs. We are not in the business to sell our clients one time. We want to develop long-term relationships with our client's goals as our top priority and everything else will take care of itself.

*How can someone find out more about Bob Kerr and Living Sky Marketing, LTD and how you can help?*

**Robert Kerr**: You can find out more about Bob Kerr and Living Sky Marketing at livingskymarketing.com or just reach out to me, Bob Kerr, by phone at 306-251-0315.

For anyone interested we will always do some free research for any business to get them a snapshot of their current online presence.

## About Robert Kerr

Bob Kerr is a successful real estate investor, business owner, and entrepreneur.

Bob prides himself on operating with the highest level of integrity and enjoys serving others.

Bob is the Owner and Founder of Living Sky Marketing, which is a digital marketing firm that assists business owners in producing RESULTS with their digital marketing with his proprietary and innovative strategies.

Bob is a husband and father of 3 who enjoys helping his clients solve the complex maze of digital marketing to produce incredible results.

**BUSINESS NAME**
Living Sky Marketing

## WEBSITE
LivingSkyMarketing.com

## FACEBOOK
Facebook.com/LivingskyApps/

## LINKEDIN
Linkedin.com/in/Bob-Kerr-a2248197

# Spicer

D.A. Garcia is the founder of Syndgar Trading Company, a Spicer, and an up and coming culinary entrepreneur and educator to thousands of people on the properties of natural herbs and spices. At the Syndgar Trading Company D.A. creates custom spice and herb seasoning blends using one-hundred percent natural ingredients that serve as delicious and healthy alternatives to the many popular synthetic-laced spices sitting on grocery store shelves today. D.A. enjoys sharing his vast knowledge and new research via daily live broadcasts on Facebook and has helped countless individuals improve the quality of their diet and the quality of their lives.

D.A. is also a U.S. Marine Corps and U.S. Army combat veteran that actively supports fellow veteran entrepreneurs with his business acumen, education and experience. In short, D.A. Garcia is very much a modern-day renaissance man and story-teller practicing a centuries old craft and sharing the tales of the ingredients behind it.

# Conversation with D.A. Garcia

*David, you are the owner/operator of Syndgar Trading Co.
Tell us a little about it and how you are helping your
customers.*

**D.A. Garcia**: The Syndgar Trading Co is a reviving of a
family business that faded after WWII. My family has been in
the Texas region for generations in the "Porciones" or land
grants but as time and civilization change so did the
boundaries and means to survive. My paternal grandfather
stopped ranching and trading because he was drafted into the
Army for the Second Great War. Upon his completion of duty
from WWII as an Infantryman with the Rainbow Division he
earned a living as a tradesman in the construction industry.
My father growing up in a larger town continued to work as a
laborer and through the courtship of my mother found his way
to Chicago where she had moved with her parents. Growing
up I did not know much of my family history and I would
have thought that the forgotten business would have just
stayed forgotten. Through research I discovered that my
ancestors did more than just move cattle but arrived as
colonizers, merchants, and landowners to move goods between
The New World and Spain. After my family history was
verified I was hooked and decided to continue with what feels
right in my blood.

I assist my customers in the providing of spices, herbs, and
other fine items with the purest of ingredients and materials
available. I believe that with the lifestyle of immediate
gratification people have forgotten that family and tradition
are important. The family meals, gatherings, and fellowships

of loved ones have been replaced with lost time through modern conveniences. By providing customers with an aroma to create memories and tastes that brings people home the happiness of bonding will be rekindled to allow values and time well spent together to thrive in the home.

*What a great background story for a company. Describe at least one big problem you specialize in solving.*

**D.A. Garcia**: Creating the exposure needed to get the products noticed. Most people are addicted to the heavy sodium and sugar tastes of quick meals. The same ingredients added to make people's meals a quick fix is also the same ingredients that harm their health but without the right exposure people will not know that. The Syndgar Trading Co. is around with their best savory interests in mind.

That's great that you are providing healthier alternatives without making folks sacrifice on taste. What's the outcome that can be achieved by working with you and your products.

The movement to healthier lifestyles through wellness is already in action and most people are aware of what can be achieved through finding what whole foods can achieve in their lives, but spices and herbs are not usually paid attention to when adjusting eating habits. People will throw away cabinets of food and empty their refrigerators in hopes of creating a new food regime but forget the spices. They hold onto heavily sodium based dry rubs, preservative pack mixes, or bottles filled with anti-caking agents that are not natural to ingest. Working with The Syndgar Trading Co is a movement to create awareness that lifestyle adjustments are not just in the foods but the additives to the foods. When further awareness if made by us and the benefits to whole and sourced blends we can offer our products first.

*Please describe the difference taking this whole of diet approach can make in someone's life.*

**D.A. Garcia**: Only a positive outcome can be had by choosing sourced and whole herbs, spices, and minerals are all the additional ingredients added to blends are not necessary for both health and budget. Through each order placed with us the customer is getting the full blend of herbs, spices, and minerals meaning that they receive more for their money, but that is secondary to the quality that they are adding to their individual wellness. Ingesting natural and whole blends provides the full benefits of each ingredient that nature intended.

*What are some of the advantages of including all-natural spice blends in a person's diet?*

**D.A. Garcia**: The benefit is the allowance of the ingredients to be worked into the body without interference with synthetic agents. Similar to the idea of watering down a solution to break the concentration down. Tastes, aroma, and benefits are lost to outside chemicals when added to a mix to achieve unnecessary shelf life or act as a filler for larger companies to save money by volume.

*What do you feel are the biggest myths out there when it comes to the value of consciously including all natural spices in a person's eating regimen?*

**D.A. Garcia**: The learned behavior of common tastes. Most Western diets have palates destroyed by a fast lifestyle. Eating on-the-go and a meal in the home of microwave and oven heated meals coated in preservatives and sodium provide the illusion of salt as a main ingredient. Sugar coated snacks, cereals, and drinks trick the mind to only want a sweet taste. The mix of sweet and salt provide most people from feeling that if they add the wonderful additions of other natural ingredients that they will miss taste or not enjoy the meal. The other side of the coin is that if they were to add these ingredients that the costs would not be worth the purchase and other ingredients are for an upper class. The low costs of sugar and salt which were premium at one time are very affordable and a 25lbs bag of salt cost less than a one-pound bag of black pepper. Breaking the barrier of cost and benefits is the best way to bring value back to the public's eating regime.

*What are some common misconceptions around some of the more well-known spices?*

**D.A. Garcia**: The popularity of each bigger name based on location in the markets. As eye-level placements and availability to reduce prices based on quantity distract the customers from the actual ingredients. When the subject of health over immediate is discussed most consumers rather pay a lower cost now to achieve a cheaper alternative yet when the health issues arrive are shocked at the price of medications to stymie or temporarily aid against disease or illness from years of ingesting of too many synthetics. Well-known spices may have natural ingredients but when too many unnecessary ingredients are added the benefits are lost and the costs are more than dollars down the road.

*What are some of the most common fears about natural remedies?*

**D.A. Garcia**: One is "What if it doesn't work?" To that all I can say is there are not guaranteed cures for anything. Similar to adjusting the color on a picture a person is either taking away or adding "green" over "red." The same will happen with an illness. People look for immediate results for everything, back to the immediate gratification of society. Someone wants to lose weight overnight he or she starves themselves hurting the body. They endure hours of cardio and lose muscle mass. Everything should be done as routine. If the lifestyle changes the "cures" will be easier to achieve from the healthy routines.

Some people worry about "What others would think about me making such a big deal about all-natural spices and the extra cost?" All I can tell you is that everyone one who has tried our blends have been happy and love not only the excellent aroma of the mixtures of our ingredients but also the popping of flavor from each meal that leaves a positive impression. Customers have told me on many occasions of their children who are often picky eaters or dabblers eat each bite with a smile, leftovers are never a problem. We do not claim to cure any ailments but do inform of the benefits of what a natural ingredient can bring into a person's life, meaning we are not selling a hope to cure but an excellent way to reap the benefits from what nature has intended for each person who chooses to use plants and minerals in their meals.

And there are a small minority that are concerned about damaging side effects. However, the only risk is if the person who uses are blends are allergic to any of the natural ingredients within the blends. That is why we include an ingredient list on the website and do not add anything not on the list.

*What other perceived obstacles do you see that might be preventing more people from enjoying the benefits of natural herb, spice and mineral blends on their diet?*

**D.A. Garcia**: The two main factors are knowledge and cost. If people do not know about the product they will not be able to find our selections. Then cost, but with the right knowledge about why quality and natural ingredients might be a bit pricier than synthetics price will no longer be an obstacle.

We include an ingredient list with our products and offer free knowledge through our Facebook group The Spice Traveler's Circle to inform the public of what natural blends can do for them as well as our ingredients. Also, with the release of our International Best-Selling Book 'The Spice Traveler' an audience can read what exactly and why we chose the nine ingredients for our Specialty Select Blend, "Raider."

*What are some of the little-known pitfalls or common mistakes you see when people do decide to try natural remedies and supplements?*

**D.A. Garcia**: They overdo the task. Most people rush out and buy everything they can and spend over their budget hoping for an immediate gain then get discourage and forget about everything. The situation usually leads to an "all or nothing" scenario causing regret and resentment toward the original goal. Planning is needed as well as patience. Just add the ingredients and enjoy life, celebrate each small win and make the habits forming into a lifestyle.

*How can these mistakes be avoided?*

**D.A. Garcia**: Plan and appreciate. If the person makes a plan and appreciates the smallest of victories happiness will follow to become routine then habit and a lifestyle is created.

*Can you share an example of how you have helped your customers overcome these obstacles and succeed in enjoying the physical and mental benefits of including natural spice blends in their diet?*

Aside from myself I would say that the hardest customers to convince were my parents. I find in my family a child trying to change the habits of his parents is hard. My parents were hourly workers during my childhood years and they retired with nearly 40 years each in their respected unions. They had many habits developed from "babyboomers"/ "Jones" generations with synthetic, salt, sugar, and butter being their go-to flavors in the kitchen. Yes, they would use other ingredients from time to time but not without the heavy mix of the sodium or sweet flavors. Over 55 years of habit was quickly broken down along with the illnesses they developed to include diabetes and high blood pressure through my education of natural inclusion into my meals. My testimonies to eliminating synthetics and use of natural ingredients encouraged them to my blends which created new advocates to The Syndgar Trading Co. not because they are my parents but because they believe in my products.

*What inspired you to become a "Spicer"?*

**D.A. Garcia**: Prior to knowing my family history, I was tired of my body hurting and the medications given to me from doctors. I was gaining unnecessary weight, blacking out more often, feeling horrible, and just hating life. I was attempting to find my own ways from the art of herbalism. I found an old Readers Digest in my library that my mother gave me, and I began my research to find a means to living a better life. Eventually my elixirs led to dry rubs and today I have developed several blends to achieve not only excellent companions to meals but a stronger life.

*David, what drives you and your passion to do what you do and help the people you help.*

**D.A. Garcia**: I am a gamer at heart, I played table top and video games for many years and I love fantasy. Each character I played always has a magic elixir that heals him when really hurt. Once the Elder Scroll series was introduced to me I was hooked on the notion of elixirs. While I was in the Marines I was considering using my GI Bill to enroll as a Pharmacy Tech to learn about prescribed medications and biochemistry. My apartment had different herb and spice plants and I was trying to make my own little mixes for fun. Many years later, after being fed up with my own prescribed medications I remembered this small passion and began my own little lab in the house. I have been hooked ever since. Many years in the making.

*Can you share a lesson you learned early on, that still impacts how you do business today?*

**D.A. Garcia**: Honor. Always keep your word and be honest. A man is nothing without his word. Honor is actually embedded into my values: Family, Honor, and Tradition

*What was the biggest obstacle you had to overcome to start your journey as a professional spicer?*

**D.A. Garcia**: That I would not be good enough. With so many celebrities and showmen in culinary especially with the rise of kitchen/cooking shows on every network I doubted myself. I find it funny now-a-days as I am very confident in not only each blend that I create but in The Syndgar Trading Co. As long as I remain true to our goals and values I will overcome each obstacle.

*What's the most important question a consumer should ask themselves about the foods and medications they are currently ingesting?*

**D.A. Garcia**: Am I allergic to this ingredient? Am I currently taking something that will counteract the active ingredients to this blend?

*What's the most important thing should consider when specifically evaluating spices to include in their diet?*

**D.A. Garcia**: Taste and agreeable to the body. Do you enjoy the taste? Would your body reject the ingredient?

*Thanks for talking with me David. How can someone find out more about D. A. Garcia and Syndgar Trading Co. and how you can help?*

**D.A. Garcia**: There are a few places. You can find us at our website: SyndgarTradingCo.com, join our Facebook Group at The Spice Travelers Circle and I invite everyone to read the interesting story behind my very first spice blend in my bestselling Amazon Kindle book *The Spice Traveler.*

# About D.A. Garcia

D.A. Garcia is the founder and Chief Operating Officer of Syndgar Trading Company where he manages the accounts between Syndgar Corporation and manufacturers and wholesalers in The United States, Canada, Spain, Mexico, Thailand, India, and Africa.

D.A.'s favorite role at Syndgar Trading Company Supervise is the research and development of new product lines. Particularly the production and monitoring of culinary creations for the company's dry spice line.

David has enjoyed a varied and accomplished life serving in both the U.S. Marine Corps and U.S. Army; as a security professional to Hollywood stars, running his own private security company; as a Stevedore; becoming a Certified Jeweler through the Gemological Institute of America; and earning his MBA in Accounting and Business Activities at the John Sperling School of Business. Additionally, D.A. recently became an Amazon International Bestselling Author with his book "The Spice Traveler"

Today D.A. Garcia runs Syndgar Trading Company with his wife Nicy Garcia from their ranch in the Brownwood Texas area.

**WEBSITE**
SyndgarTradingCo.com

**LINKEDIN**
LinkedIn.com/in/David-A-Garcia-830a679/

**FACEBOOK**
Facebook.com/SyndgarTradingCo

# SW Florida Real Estate Expert

Christian Fautz, JD is an entrepreneur by nature having worked for himself at an early age where he had his first paper route at nine years old, to start a health food company while in college. Christian is always seeking to increase his knowledge of real estate investing and staying on top of market trends. He continues to develop strategic partners to expand his real estate investing throughout Florida.

# Conversation With Christian Fautz, JD

*Tell us about Core Real Estate Properties and how you are helping your clients.*

**Christian Fautz:** Core Real Estate Properties is one of Fort Myers and South West Florida's premier real estate investment groups. We are professional home buyers that buy houses that are off-market which means they are not currently listed with a real estate agent or through an MLS service. We specialize in helping people explore different options on how to best sell their house quickly.

We follow several Core Values that are essential to how we conduct our real estate business:

1.  A Problem Solver: We pride ourselves on being able to offer viable solutions and think outside of the box to help our clients find solutions that meet their needs and objectives.
2.  Transparency: We promise to conduct ourselves with open, honest and direct communications which allows us and you to make informed decisions.
3.  Empathetic: We do our best to understand your challenges and concerns to be able to better and more effectively provide solutions to help you meet them.
4.  Accountability: We make a commitment to deliver what we promise.
5.  Community: Part of our culture is to give back to our community; to make a difference in people's lives when they most need it.

6. Respect: We each command respect and we each show respect, it is a principle we strive to conduct in all our real estate dealings.

*Describe at least one big problem you specialize in solving.*

**Christian Fautz:** When people go to sell their house there are two unknowns always involved in the process; when are they going to sell it; and for how much? We take the uncertainty out of the process when sellers work with us by giving them our best offer. When selling as-is, you do not have to worry about negotiations after the home inspection process because if we do one, it is done before we make an all-cash offer. Second, we give them a firm date on when we can close. Along with eliminating the uncertainty of the sales process, they do not have to go through the hassles of making repairs, upgrades, cleaning or staging of their house. Our offers are never contingent on the seller making any repairs.

*Describe the outcome that can be achieved by working with you.*

**Christian Fautz:** Our sellers know exactly what we will pay right away and once we agree on a price that is what we will buy it for. We also include in most of our offers to pay the closing costs and all transfer fees so our clients do not have to spend any money to sell their home. We make the transaction as seamless as possible.

*Describe the difference in achieving this outcome can make in their life.*

**Christian Fautz:** Working with a real estate investor, you will know that you have your house sold right away. This allows Sellers to have peace of mind and avoid the possibility of having to pay ongoing expenses for a house they no longer want or maybe can't afford. It may also keep them from going into foreclosure if they are behind on mortgage payments and further damaging their credit.

*What are the advantages of selling their home quickly for Home Sellers?*

**Christian Fautz:** Time and Money are two key advantages to selling your home quickly to a professional house buying company like Core Real Estate Properties. If you ask any investor they will tell you that the longer you own a house, the more it will cost you. Every day you are the owner, you are paying your mortgage, utilities, taxes, insurance and maintenance costs. When you look at the ongoing monthly expenses and any repairs needed to make your house more marketable all the bills can add up pretty quickly. By selling your house quickly, you will be able to immediately start saving by eliminating these costs now instead of months down the road.

When you try to sell your house traditionally through an agent it can take both time and money. First, you have to pay commission to your real estate agent. Second, you most likely will have to make repairs that will cost you both time and money. Third, most buyers today along with their mortgage lender require a home inspection to be performed. And once your potential buyer has the home inspection done, they will more likely than not either negotiate that any necessary repairs be made by the seller or request a reduction in the sales price.

*What do you feel are the biggest myths out there when it comes to homeowners to sell their home quickly?*

**Christian Fautz:** It is the same size fits all mentality when selling a home. There is no one-size fits all solution to sell your home especially for those people who need to sell quickly. There are many ways to sell your house. What works for one property, may not work for another. Some properties do phenomenally well being marketed by a real estate agent on the MLS and sell quickly, while others sit on the market for months with no signs of a potential sale.

For some sellers, the time and potential cost simply aren't worth it. In addition, to paying the agents commission and fees, you will also have to spend money making repairs, cleaning and staging the house. Don't forget the stress of having to always keep the house clean for those last minute showings and the uncertainty of what type of repairs a home inspection report may uncover. For some people, none of this is a problem. They have the time to wait around and don't have many repairs to make on the home. Other sellers do not have this luxury.

Another method is for-sale-by-owner. FSBO can be a lot of work, especially if you are unfamiliar with the process. Selling your own home to a buyer who wants to live there can take time and require a lot of work from you. That said, in certain situations, and for people who understand the sales process, an FSBO can be another viable selling option by utilizing real estate sites such as Zillow or realtor.com.

Many sellers find themselves waiting for an offer for a certain price that none of these selling options can provide. Many people, especially those who purchased before the bubble burst, will hold out, expecting to get what they originally paid for their house. Yes, the real estate market throughout the U.S. and especially in the State of Florida have rebounded since the last recession. Unfortunately, depending on your local real estate market, this isn't always the case. If it has come down to this, you can either cut your losses and walk away, or continue holding on to a house you don't really want or can't afford anymore.

An alternative way to go maybe with a real estate investor who can explore with the seller different options and help make a smart decision on how to sell their home fast and at a fair price.

*What are some common misconceptions about the Real Estate Industry?*

**Christian Fautz:** I believe one of the biggest misconceptions is that when you sell your home to a real estate investor at a lower price it should be the last option you look at. You might be reading this and asking yourself why would anyone accept below market price for their house? That's a good question; however, there is more to the story.

In the real estate industry, most people do not understand that there are really two different real estate markets There is the most common one that everyone knows and understands which is the "on the market" real estate. When a house is sold "on the market," it means you're selling it to a person who will choose to live in the house. Selling "on the market" usually means the buyer needs to obtain financing. Approval of financing takes time and can be a contingency in the contract which could hinder the closing of your house.

On market houses are generally listed by a real estate agent and marketed through the MLS. The agent will usually have a serious of open houses for both potential buyers and other real estate agents. The goal is to obtain an offer and enter into a contract for the purchase of the home. Generally, houses sold "on the market" will often be sold in the same neighborhood for approximately the same amount that other houses in a similar condition have sold for which is referred to as the market price.

The second less known option to sell your house is in the "off-market" real estate. When selling "off-market" the homeowner enters into a private sale with a real estate investor or professional home buying company such as Core Real Estate Properties. Most real estate investors pay cash or have their financing in place to close on the sale quickly. They generally will buy your home as-is and prefer to buy homes that need repairs or renovations. Since houses sold "off market" are being sold as-is and in a short amount of time they will often be sold for less than their market price what is referred to as below market price.

When you sell "off-market" there is no emotional side of the sale since they are not buying the house for themselves and their family. The house is being purchased to turn it into a rental property or to renovate it and sell it.

*What are some of the most common fears about selling their home?*

**Christian Fautz:** It's similar to some of the misconceptions I discussed about selling your home "on the market" compared to selling it "off market." I believe there are fears associated either way you end up selling your home. The fear of selling "on the market" is how long will it take; am I going to get my price; and will I be able to sell my house without having to spend a lot of money making repairs? The fears associated with selling off-market boils down to one: how much am I going to have to discount the price of my house to sell it now.

*Beyond their ability?*

**Christian Fautz:** If you go the traditional route of selling your house by listing it with a real estate agent once you sign the listing agreement it is pretty much out of your hands as you wait for an offer. However, if you sell directly to a real estate investor you know exactly what the investor will pay right away. You have control over the sales process and do not have to accept their offer but I see it as a good first step to help you decide how you want to move forward in selling your house.

*What if it doesn't work?*

**Christian Fautz:** If listing your house for sale on market does not work you have lost both time and money. You may find that you have to repeatedly lower the price to get your house sold. Potential buyers will take note of these price reductions which could give them the impression that something is wrong with the house or that you are desperate to sell. In this case, you may have been better to sell your house from the start directly to a real estate investor saving time and money.

What would others think?
Damaging side effects?
Personal risk?

*How can they get past these fears?*

**Christian Fautz:** Sellers need to be informed and do their research. Go back to the key questions I summarized previously and be sure to answer them before deciding on how to best sell your home. This will allow you to weigh the benefits of what is best for you when considering to sell. Selling your house at market price may not always be the highest price if you factor in the time it may take to sell along with the expenses associated with it such as commissions, closing costs, possible repairs and the monthly expenses of owning your home.

*What other perceived obstacles do you see that might be preventing home sellers from seeking the help of a Real Estate Investor?*

**Christian Fautz:** I believe the biggest obstacle is trust. People who have to sell their house in a short amount of time generally need to do so because of a number of different reasons. They may be having financial difficulties due to the loss of a job, or maybe due to health issues that have caused them to suffer financially. In other instances, maybe they have inherited property that is in another State that is vacant or is not being properly managed. The heirs want to sell it fast so that the estate can be settled. I have also seen houses that are part of a divorce proceeding that must sell quickly so that the divorce can be finalized. In many of these cases, the sellers prefer to sell to a real estate investor rather than waiting for the house to be sold "on the market."

The perception is that when you sell your property to an investor is that they are going to take advantage of your position and try to buy your house for pennies on the dollar.

However, that does not have to be the case. When you work with the right investor, you will receive a fair price for your house. You will be able to sell right away instead of months down the road and you will be able to sell it without having to spend money making repairs. Of course, not all real estate investors are the same. Make sure you are working with an experienced, trusted home buyer such as our company, Core Real Estate Properties, who will deal honestly and openly with you.

*What are some of the little-known pitfalls or common mistakes you see Home Sellers make on the road to sell their home quickly?*

**Christian Fautz:** Not understanding the different options available to sell their home and the benefits of selling their home now in its current condition. As I have previously stated, it is important for a home seller to do their research and understand all the costs associated with selling their home. There are real costs. Once they have the information then they can weigh the benefits of selling their home as-is to a real estate investor at a discounted price rather than listing it for sale with no guarantee when or for how much it will sell for.

*How can these pitfalls / mistakes be avoided?*

**Christian Fautz:** A home seller can avoid the mistake of having their house sit on the market for months at a time by meeting with a professional home buying company such Core Real Estate Properties at the beginning of your decision to sell your home. A real estate investor will be able to quickly let you know how much they will buy your home for before you decide to list it for sale. This way a seller with an offer in hand you can evaluate your options.

They should also research or ask a local real estate agent how long the average home in their area has taken to sell. A real estate agent can provide a competitive market analysis (CMA) for the seller which will provide a reasonable expectation on how much their house could sell for by listing it and how long it may take.

*Can you share an example of how you have helped your clients overcome these obstacles and succeed in selling their home quickly?*

**Christian Fautz:** I had a seller contact me through our website. He had relocated to another State for work but still owned a home in South West Florida. He listed his home with a local real estate agent before he moved. It had been on the market for several months with no offers. He told me that he was having difficulty keeping up with the expenses of owning two homes. He did not want to fall behind on his payments and jeopardize his good credit.

I knew this area has a high demand for seasonal rentals during the winter months so I asked him if he tried to rent the house seasonally to earn some income to offset his expenses?

He told me that it was difficult to find a renter without having the house furnished since he moved all his furnishings to his new home? Once I gathered all the information, I made arrangements to see it. It was in good condition but needed some cosmetic updates.

I asked the owner if he was willing to do some cosmetic work, and also professionally stage it to help market it? He told me that he did not have the funds to invest nor could he continue to pay the monthly expenses for more than another month or two. We worked out a solution with him where we would take over his payments for him and invest the necessary funds to make the repairs and professionally stage the home in return for a discounted price. We ended up selling the house within a few months and helped the seller avoid having his credit damaged by falling behind on his monthly payments. In the end, this was a win-win situation for both the seller and our company.

*What inspired you to become a Real Estate Investor?*

**Christian Fautz:** I received my law degree from the St. John's University School of Law in New York. While in law school, I interned for a local law firm. The law firm specialized in landlord/tenant and bankruptcy law. During my internship, I did a lot of the intake work with the clients to prepare the necessary paperwork to file their bankruptcy petition. I gathered their personal and financial information along with listening to their story on how the ended up in this position. There were many sad stories that I witnessed first hand of the financial hardships that families can go through due to the loss of a job, death of a family member, a divorce or even from a prolonged illness.

In many of the bankruptcy cases, I worked on the people had their house in foreclosure or were close to it. They were going to lose their home under their bankruptcy case. I asked many of them if they had tried to sell their house before the foreclosure proceedings or decided to file for bankruptcy? Many of them had not and those that did said their house sat on the market for months while the bills continued to mount up. This experience planted the seed that inspired me to start Core Real Estate Properties to help people learn and explore different options on how to best sell their house quickly.

When I first started out working with homeowners looking to sell their home to my real estate company, I sometimes found myself hesitating in making them an offer. I felt that maybe what I was willing to pay was going to be much lower than what they expected. I did not want them to perceive me as that home buyer making them a low-ball offer.

I overcame this misconception one day during a meeting with a seller. I was sitting with them in their living room and they asked me to make them an offer as they told me that they felt comfortable working with me. I reviewed with them what I could pay for their home and how I came up with the amount based on my analysis. They understood that I was providing a solution to their need to sell their house quickly and my open communication helped them make a decision to sell to my company. I learned that by being open and honest in presenting my offers is just as important as the amount of the offer.

*Can you share a lesson you learned early on, that still impacts how you do business today?*

**Christian Fautz:** Educating and providing people with options is the best way to conduct your business. I had a homeowner that I met with who was looking to sell his house but was unsure of how to best sell it. I explained to him the different methods including trying to sell it for the market price with a real estate agent which could yield him a higher price but also may take more time. He told me had some time but wanted to know if he did not sell it in a few months would my offer still be open. I told him yes, wished him the best with selling his home and asked him to keep me updated. A few months later he called me and told me he was successful in selling his house. He thanked me because knowing that he had a backup offer with me provided him the opportunity to see if he could sell his house for a higher price. I learned that being transparent and educating people will always yield you the best result. Yes, this did not end up with me buying their house, however, I have had other instances where because of this transparency, the seller came back and sold me their house for my original offer.

*What's the most important question home sellers should ask themselves as they consider selling their home?*

**Christian Fautz:** Most people who sell their house just decide to sell it without thinking through what it looks like. I believe it is important for sellers to do research ahead of time and ask questions to be more informed about the process of selling their home. Some important questions to ask are:

* How much should I sell my house for so that it is priced right in the marketplace?

* What happens if the listing takes a long time for the house to sell?
* Do you have a budget for the ongoing expenses and any repairs needed?
* If repairs are needed, how long will they take to get done?
* What contingencies do you have if the real estate agent can't find a buyer?

*What's the most important thing home sellers should consider when evaluating a Real Estate Investor?*

**Christian Fautz:** Are they going to treat you fairly, honestly along with their ability to close quickly without any contingencies? I also believe it is important whether they are a local real estate investor or a national investor. The reason is your local investor will understand the local real estate market better than the national investor and will often offer a better price. The typical national real estate investor cast a wide net making low ball offers with the understanding that the majority of their offers will get rejected but the ones that don't will be at rock bottom prices. As a local real estate investor, we take the time to meet with our seller clients. Core Real Estate Properties specializes in working with sellers in Southwest Florida and has key strategic local partners they work with throughout Florida.

*Describe what drives you and your passion to do what you do and help the people you help.*

**Christian Fautz:** I enjoy helping people find solutions to problems they may be facing when selling their home. By taking the time to listen and understand their situation I can better find out how I may be able to help them.

*How can someone find out more about Christian Fautz, JD and Core Real Estate Properties and how you can help?*

**Christian Fautz:** You can find out more about me, my company and the different type of real estate services we provide by visiting CoreRealEstateProperties.com and to learn how we can help sell your house quickly visit SellYourHouseNowUSA.com.

You can also contact me at (800) 455-5458 or by email at Christian@corerealestateproperties.com with any questions. At Core Real Estate Properties we think of ourselves as your trusted real estate partner and hold ourselves to a high standard of integrity, transparency and to deal fairly in all our business dealings.

## About Christian Fautz, JD

Christian Fautz, JD is an entrepreneur by nature having worked for himself at an early age where he had his first paper route at nine years old, to start a health food company while in college. Christian is always seeking to increase his knowledge of real estate investing and staying on top of market trends. He continues to develop strategic partners to expand his real estate investing throughout Florida.

He graduated from The George Washington University and has a law degree from St. John's University. He owns multi-family properties, wholesales properties, rehabs and flips single-family homes and has invested in real estate internationally where he helped develop a residential real estate project in Costa Rica that was featured on HGTV International. He is a licensed real estate agent in Florida where he is an active real estate investor and works in construction management doing residential remodeling. He conducts his business by providing clients with open, honest and direct communications. By better understanding their challenges and concerns, he believes is the best way to be able to effectively provide the right solution.

He currently resides in sunny South West Florida with his family. He is the proud Dad of Eden and relishes time with his beautiful wife. He enjoys spending time playing golf and boating with family and friends. He can be reached at christian@corerealestateproperties.com or at (800) 455-5458. To learn more about his company visit:

**BUSINESS NAME**
Core Real Estate Properties

**WEBSITE**
CoreRealEstateProperties.com
SellYourHouseNowUSA.com
BuyOffMarketRealEstate.com

**FACEBOOK**
Facebook.com/SellingAndBuyingRealEstate

www.ingramcontent.com/pod-product-compliance
Lightning Source LLC
Chambersburg PA
CBHW050120210326
41519CB00015BA/4045